HAPPY

Birthday

- Macy

HAPPY

Birthday

-Macy

F Y P

Fuck Your Past

Tzachi Ozeri

F YP
Fuck Your Past

First Edition: 2022

ISBN: 9781524316938
ISBN eBook: 9781524328009

© of the text:
   Tzachi Ozeri

© Layout, design and production
   of this edition: 2022 EBL

Table of Contents

Introduction

Like so many of us during the pandemic, I lost everything. Three opportunities just slipped through my fingers, two work related and the other to do with love.

When lockdown first hit, we all had so much time to ourselves that it was a novelty. This freedom to do nothing was fun and relaxing, and I loved the chance to kick back and unwind.

But gradually, just like before, I slipped into a mundane routine. It might have been different from when I was working outside of my home, but it was a routine nevertheless—and with less freedom, not more. A typical day looked something like this:

- Wake up.
- Maybe go to the gym.
- Coffee at the local bakery.
- Work.
- Have an after-hours drink.
- Go to the gym, practice yoga, or watch a movie on Netflix.
- Sleep.

This routine was how I adapted to the new normal, which still had just as much overthinking, stress, and overwhelm as before, never knowing when things would end, not knowing when businesses would open up again or if I'd get sick the next day. This promising opportunity to start all over again and build a new structure for my life began to feel annoying and lost its meaning.

I know I'm not the only one who went through this process. I hear it all the time from my friends and family and on social media.

But through it all, the one thing that amazed me was that my mind wasn't all that stressed for some reason. It was like it needed that time off.

My mind needed to restructure itself. The way of life I'd had before wasn't taking me anywhere I wanted to go.

Then I read a book called *The Universe Has Your Back* by Gabby Bernstein. It made me completely rethink what I was doing. I'd been skeptical about the book at first because it seemed like just another manifestation book. I mean, we've all tried it out at some point. So many people claim that all you have to do is ask the Universe for what you want, and it will provide. It can't be that simple, can it?

Well, it is, and it isn't. That book opened my eyes to a new, better way of doing things, and I was inspired to share my discoveries with you.

Now, you might be asking yourself what makes this different from all those other manifestation books. What could I possibly have to say that you haven't heard yet? What makes this a new approach?

Well, you're going to need to see that for yourself. All I ask is that you give me the chance to prove to you that it *does* work.

Before we move on to the first chapter, I want to let you know that while I'm here to help you find your own way of manifesting what you want, it doesn't matter whether you are working with G-D, Jesus, Muhammed, or the Universe. All that matters is that you believe in *something*—and believe in yourself.

I've written this book to help you, and what is most important to me is that I help as many people as possible. In fact, my goal is to help thirty million people by donating 18 percent of any profit I make from this book to those who need help. (And if you're wondering why 18 percent and not a round number like 20, we'll be going into that in more detail later in the book.)

I've discovered that my purpose in life is to help those who can't help themselves, without judgment. It's not my business to know why someone can't help themselves unless they want to share their story with me.

Whether you like my book or not, please know that by purchasing it, you're already doing good by supporting me to help those millions of people who can't afford food or medical care.

Many of us reach a point in our lives when we look around at what we've got and realize that we're unsatisfied and unfulfilled. Yet instead of doing something to change it, we let ourselves believe that this is the way life should be. We tell ourselves, "It is what it is" or "That's just how life goes," setting ourselves up to accept less than we deserve and be OK with this feeling of dissatisfaction and lack of accomplishment.

Well, excuse me while I shout, "You should never settle for less!" Full stop, period, end of story.

One of the biggest disservices you can do is allow yourself to feel that wherever you are, you've hit the limit of your ability. *There is no limit.*

I remember being told early on in my career that when you feel like you can do a better job than your boss, it's time to step up and make a change. I would add to that that when you feel you've gone as far as you can, it's time to look in a new direction.

So, before we start digging into the manifestation techniques, I'm going to share with you, I want you to start thinking about what might be blocking you. What's stopping you from embracing that innate need to delve deeper and rise higher?

How would you react if I told you that you can achieve more than you currently have, so much more? Do you believe me, or do you think that you couldn't possibly improve your life because "it is what it is"?

Trust me. We can all have more, and as soon as you see the light—which is your drive to want more than what you currently have—you will be able to bring those things into your life. And when I say more, I don't mean material things. Our reason for being is to live a *fulfilled* life. The only reason you're not achieving this is fear.

In this book, I'm going to open your mind and allow you to dig deeper into your past to discover that your issues are not because of one breakup, job loss, difficult experience, or trauma. Instead, I'm going to open your eyes to finding your purpose in life, uncovering your deepest yearnings to connect with your light, and help you find a true understanding of the best way for you to approach life and your issues.

By the time you've finished working through this book, you'll be able to see the big picture instead of holding onto the past or those obstacles we all have in our way. Our obstacles come in different shapes and sizes, depending on our personal circumstances, but whatever they are, they can be overcome. Some people are able to move past them easily, while others ignore them or allow them to rule their life. The truth is we can *all* move past them easily if we allow ourselves. The obstacles you face are not an insurmountable wall. It's simply you avoiding or fearing change.

In this book, I'm going to share with you my knowledge and experiences. I'll show you how I was able to see the signs the Universe sends all of us on a daily basis. Now, I'm not going to say it was an easy journey for me, because it certainly wasn't, but hopefully with my help, it'll be a little easier for you.

Hang in there because the difficulties will be worth it. You'll see.

*Not everything that we face can
be changed, but nothing can be
changed until it is faced.*

—James Baldwin

1

I want to start by telling you a story of what happened to me when I was around twenty-two years old. As soon as I left the army, I wanted to upgrade my high school grades, so I went back to school.

After leaving class one day, I went to the nearest bus stop. It was full of kids like me who had just finished their classes. As I was waiting, a woman got up from her seat and asked me when the last bus to where she needed to go would arrive.

"You just missed it," I said.

She replied, "Oh well. I'll walk."

Seeing me about to leave, she handed me her ticket for the bus. At the time, free-pass tickets for the bus were marked "female" or "male." So, I told her, "Thank you, but I have my own and can't use yours since you are female and I'm male."

She smiled at me and said, "Wow, you're a very detail-focused person."

I smiled back. "Not really; it's just a fact that I'm male."

Instead of leaving, she asked me, "What is your name and date of birth?"

"Why?" I asked.

"Don't be scared," was her cryptic reply.

"I'm not," I said. "It's just a weird question from someone I don't know." However, something prompted me to give her my name and date of birth.

Now, I'm going to be honest. I don't remember everything she told me after I answered her questions. What I *do* remember is the feeling I had. Afterward, I rushed to call my mom because I was so scared and nervous after hearing what she told me.

Now remember—I didn't know this woman. I'd never seen her before. But when I gave her my name and date of birth, she started talking about my past in a very detailed way. She mentioned my mom and dad and their struggles. She told me I should stop blaming myself for their mistakes.

I asked her, "Were you following me? How do you know all this? Just from numbers?"

She told me, "Yes. That's what I do."

I remember her getting onto my bus, which wasn't the same one she had been asking about earlier. On the bus, she asked what I was planning to study. At the time, I was planning to go to fashion school. I remember she told me that this was not where I belonged. She told me I should study law and added a few other options that I don't remember.

Before she got off two stops later, she said, "If you want your life to change, add the letter *a* in between the other letters of your name."

I told her that was impossible because of the way my name is pronounced and spelled in my language.

She replied, "There is a way, and you need to figure it out. Do that, and you will see your future."

At this point, I was freaking out and called my mom, asking her how the f—k any of this was possible. (You'll be pleased to hear my mom excused my language because of my shock!)

Ever since then, I started to use the English spelling of my name and added an *a* to become Tzachi. Now people simply call me Zach.

At the end of this book, I will share a secret with you that will really make you think. This book might seem like all the other law of attraction books, but I promise you it is not. You might find some of the things I'm going to share difficult to believe. I understand. I've been there myself.

But maybe my story will open your mind and make you see things differently, or even prompt you to try again at something that didn't work in the past. When you discover that secret, you'll reconsider why things didn't work before and know why they will work now. My secret will make you believe that *anything* is possible!

I will show you step by step how I saw my life before, what I did to change myself, and how I see my life now. I'll help you identify those blockages that are holding you back from your true potential. I'll help you understand the value of yourself, your time, and your energy.

I'm so excited to share all of this with you, so let's begin!

What Is Manifestation Really?

Manifestation is one of the universal laws. I'll save the others for another book, but regardless of whether you believe in manifestation or not, the law of attraction is constantly working for—or against—you.

We have all heard the saying "Be careful what you wish for" when it comes to negative thoughts.

"My boss is using me!"

"My partner is up to something behind my back!"

"The world is out to get me!"

These things might not be true right now, but keep thinking like that, and they soon will be. You'll start to resent your boss every time they ask you to do something, and whether they're using you or not, it'll feel like they are—which amounts to the same thing. You'll begin treating your partner as if they're cheating on you, so eventually they'll either have an affair or leave you, because who wants to stay with someone who doesn't trust them? You'll view every bad thing that happens as evidence of your belief that the world really is out to get you, and you'll ignore all the good in a downward spiral of paranoia.

See how easy it is for your thoughts to shape your reality?

Now, manifesting can be fast, but it can also take time for the Universe to get everything in order. Having a bad day isn't going to undo all of your manifestation work, but if you're constantly expecting bad things to happen, those thoughts will build up in your head, regardless of whether you're saying them out loud or not, doing damage you won't know about until it's too late. Some of these thoughts are buried really deep, embedded in your subconscious from childhood. These thoughts can take a while to uncover and reprogram, but if you do that hard work, you'll be amazed at the results.

This is what manifesting is all about: repeating to yourself the stuff that you want or how you wish to view yourself. By thinking and wishing, you start raising your vibration. This vibration goes off to tell the Universe, God, Jesus, Muhammed, or whoever you believe in, and they start working on your behalf. Watch out, because in a week, a month, four months, or a year, whenever the time is right, your desire will come true!

Now, if it's a good thing you are repeating in your head, wonderful! But if you're repeating negative and self-defeating thoughts, before you know it, you'll be back to square one, left with nothing. You'll be all alone, and not because of what someone did to you— you'll have done it to yourself. That vision you had or goal you were working toward will have disappeared — poof!

Do yourself a favor and make a commitment to yourself from this moment on that you will keep your focus on positive things you want to attract and not worry about the negative. After all, the positive thing you desire might not even happen, and it certainly won't happen if you don't manifest it.

(A point of order here: As I've mentioned before, your belief system doesn't matter. The law of attraction will work for you regardless. But for the purposes of this book, I'm going to use the term "Universe" when I'm discussing these higher powers. Feel free to substitute it with whatever term or name feels right for you.)

Angel Numbers

I'd like to take a moment to discuss the value of numbers. Numbers have incredible importance. We program our physical lives with numbers, whether it be coding for apps or computers, calculating medicine doses, playing the stock market, or earning and spending money. Numbers are all around us, yet few of us understand their secrets.

Wouldn't you like to know that you are being guided and supported every single moment of your life? Wouldn't you like to know that if you need help, you only have to ask, and help will be on its way? That's a pretty good feeling.

Our guardian angels are watching over us all the time. Your angels are always working on your behalf, whether or not you are aware of them. But they are unable to intervene directly in your affairs unless you call on them. This is why our guardian angels often communicate to us through symbolic language, images, and angel numbers.

If you are unsure about the direction your life is headed, pay close attention to the messages that are coming your way from your guardian angels. They are waiting for you.

Now, I could write an entire book about all the angel numbers and their meanings. Possibly the most famous numbers are eleven and 1,111, but I'd like to focus on one number that has held a particular resonance in my life. Maybe it's a number you've noticed around you but have never paid attention to before now. I see numbers as signs, and if you Google each number, 99 percent of the time they will give you clarity about what you need to do or where you are at in life.

I'm writing this section on November 6, 2020. My birthday. I have an annual tradition of looking up which number will guide me for the following year.

Each of us has a numerology number defined by our birthdays. Numerologists will look at your date and time of birth to calculate yours. The time of your birth is very important when calculating your future. Every minute counts because every minute shows a different path of your life.

Angel number thirty-nine is my angel number this year, which describes my past, present, and future. I was amazed at how accurate it was when I looked into the number and its meaning.

Angel Number Thirty-Nine

Angel number thirty-nine is a combination of the numbers three and nine.

The number three is a wonderfully positive number. It has a positive energy and is associated with original thought and high levels of creativity. It is an artistic number bringing with it the ability to solve problems creatively. Three is also connected to effective communication and building connections.

The number nine, or 3 x 3, takes the beautiful energy of three and takes it to the next level. It has a high vibration, meaning it is significant for your spiritual journey and is connected to the purpose you were put on this earth to fulfil.

Not only is three the square root of nine, the two numbers together are also an expression of the number three, since 3 +9 = 12 and 1 +2 = 3. This makes angel number thirty-nine an incredibly powerful number, which is likely to appear when you are searching for inspiration or looking for a sign that you are on the right path. When you see it, your angels are trying to tell you that you already have all the wisdom you need. You just have to open yourself up to receiving.

Your angels are always here to help you, so don't be afraid to ask for their help. Three in particular is connected with the ascended masters who have the power to make your dreams come true. When you see angel number thirty-nine, they are telling you that they are right there with you, happy to give you assistance.

If you're finding yourself seeing angel number thirty-nine over again, you might like to meditate on it. Sit quietly and focus on your breath until you achieve a relaxed state. Then ask yourself a question that has been bothering you, like "What is my purpose? What am I meant to do?" Then pay attention to whatever response comes to you, regardless of how crazy it may seem. Repeat this exercise over a few days, and you'll start to notice recurring themes. This is a message from your angels.

If you have been finding yourself falling into negative thoughts and patterns, now is the time for you to let these go. Focus on the positive; even the most challenging situation holds a lesson for you to learn. If you're struggling to find the positive, do those things that lift you up. Put on some happy music and dance, or sing songs at the top of your voice, no matter how out of tune.

Ask your angels to help lift you up and release those lingering resentments. They are here to tell you to never give up and look forward to the future with optimism. Good things are on the horizon for you.

Exercise

Make a list of all the places you might see an angel number. Start with the basics, like the time of day, but then get creative with things like the total on a till when you buy your groceries. When you start thinking about it, you'll realize that you're surrounded by numbers wherever you go.

Once you are aware of where you might see numbers, start paying attention to them. Is there a particular number that keeps appearing? What is its meaning?

Start journaling about the angel numbers that you see and the meanings they hold for you so that you have a record you can look over to notice how valuable these messages are.

Now that you've opened yourself up to seeing signs from the Universe, you can start manifesting little signs that you're on the right path. You might ask the Universe to send you a blue feather (which can also be a sign that Archangel Michael is nearby) or pink flowers. Make it something simple but unusual so that there's no doubt that it is a genuine sign.

Or, you might have a specific question you need an answer to. For example, if you're considering leaving your partner, ask the Universe to show you something you don't see very often if you're meant to stay together. Make it possible but unlikely so you get a clear answer, like a purple car or a rabbit running across the road. If you see it, you'll know for certain what you should do.

2

There was a time in my life when I was sleeping in a van or on a friend's sofa. Worse, I was doing drugs to relieve the pain of living my life. I wasn't ready to accept the simple truth that if I wanted to become someone, someone I could be proud of, I needed to believe I could do it, even if no one else believed in me, and I needed to help myself.

I'd managed to cut my drug use back to once a week, kidding myself that drugs were still the cure to my problems. After all, they made me feel good, and feeling good was, well, a *good* thing.

Of course, drugs weren't a cure. Sure, they let me forget the past or avoid the present for a few hours, but the reality was they made things worse. And once I managed to stop using them altogether, what was left? My thoughts. Those constant fearful thoughts were becoming stronger and stronger, manifesting a reality that was a world apart from what I really wanted to do.

The problem wasn't the drugs. It was me. That was a harsh reality to face, but while drugs allowed me to avoid facing my past, I needed to dig deep into them, understand my childhood fears so I could release the hold they had over my life once and for all. Where did those fears come from? What was my childhood like?

I had to get to the bottom of it before I could move forward.

According to my mom, my family was doing well until she fell pregnant with me. Yep. The truth hurts! But it also heals.

When I was born, Mom already had my two brothers and sister to look after. Throw a newborn into the mix, and she had a lot on her plate! As if that wasn't bad enough, after she had me, my dad left her for another woman, sold his gas business and stock, then came back to us with debts!

My mom's frustrations and unconditional love for him made my life pretty difficult, especially given the fact that my dad didn't exactly treat my mom and siblings well. I just couldn't understand why she could take him back and let him mistreat his family. Seeing my mom cry all the time didn't help either, and she was always hiding from the debt collectors who came for my dad.

There's no denying it was hard to watch. Those feelings of helplessness haunted me for years. I was just a kid. What could I do?

I remember jumping out of the back window one time because debt collectors were about to break into our apartment in the middle of the night. Fun times. Not.

There's a lot more to my childhood story, but I may leave that for my next book!

Despite all this, I still felt loved as a kid. At one point, I moved in with my grandma, which made my life a bit easier. At least there wasn't drama every day— maybe it was only once every two days. Gradually, it lessened to once a month, until eventually I was old enough to escape to the army, where I swapped one type of drama for another.

Why am I telling you all of this? Well, as a kid, watching what was going on, I felt physically and mentally sick, to the point of wanting to end my life. It was that bad. I was only eleven.

I'm telling you this because, despite it all, I was still surrounded by love from my family. When things got better between my mom and dad, I felt more and more love from them, which continues to grow even now. I'm just so proud of how they overcame their struggles.

They've told me that they still hold guilt in their hearts from the past, even though I've said over and over that I forgive them. My story shows that with the good times and the bad, you can choose where you place your focus. Now I can look back at the good times and see all the love to know that I'm OK and nothing is wrong with me! What happened was not my fault. But understand that it took me a while to reconcile with my past, and if you haven't done this difficult work yet, it *will* come back to hurt you in ways you may not even appreciate. It sure did come back to haunt me when I was thirty-eight.

Face your past, then move on. Forgive yourself and anyone else who may have hurt you.

So, for me, drugs were a cure at first, but they were also what was holding me back from reaching my potential. It took me a while to see this, but eventually I came to realize that for the past thirty-eight years, I had been acting just like my mom. Yep.

My mom has the biggest heart in the world, and she gave it to anyone, and when I say anyone, oh man, I mean anyone! My mom would give her last cent and starve or not buy herself clothes just so you have what you need, because that is who she is. There I was, acting just the same, without even knowing I was doing it. I was running about, thinking, *If I help my boss or my parents, I will do better. Give long enough and hard enough, and I will succeed!*

I thought that if I helped my girlfriend to achieve her dreams, she'd love me more in return. And no, the drugs were not helping me to feel loved because they made me feel as if I wasn't getting the attention I needed, even though she gave me more than enough. I simply couldn't see it. My judgment was clouded by the so-called cure.

Sound familiar? Not enough love? Not enough money? What is enough? When does it end?

It all ends with you! The reason someone has problems with other people is because *they have a problem with themselves.* So, for example, if you feel yourself getting jealous of someone else, ask *why* should you be jealous if somebody else drives a nice car or can go jump on a jet whenever they want? Why do you care about how this person looks or what they wear? The *only* reason you care is because you are thinking less of yourself and are not happy with yourself. Deep down, you know this to be true. Buddy, I promise, if you take the time to learn from this book, you will feel better about yourself—no, you will feel *amazing* about yourself!

Now let me ask you this: who is stopping you from getting that same car or whatever the other person has? Is it bad luck? Is it your family? Is it your best friend? Is it your partner? It is your past?

You know who it is. Say it with me! Only *you* and your mind and your thoughts are stopping you.

Just because some actions (like using drugs) are normal in your circle *doesn't make it normal.* It only means you are *normal* in your circle of friends—but you can always get new friends.

Think about famous people who are still alive or lived to be a ripe old age, and then look at the ones who died young. They all did what they loved, but some of them were able to deal with their issues, and some were not. They let the *cure*—drugs—lead them to a short path in life.

Did they die early because they were happy with themselves? I don't think so. I think the life they chose wore them down. What they enjoyed, the acting, their passion, was no fun anymore, so they used what they thought was a cure to find fun and happiness again without recognizing that the real cure lay within themselves.

Yes, drugs are fun, but—and there's always a but—the next day, those problems you tried to avoid will still be there, right?

And now those problems will be twice as big, due to the side effects of the drug. You delude yourself that you can ride out the effects of a drug. You say, "I only need a good eight-hour sleep, and I'll be back to normal. I'm good to go!" Yep, I was just like that. Hah!

This is the fucking mistake that everyone makes, because you're in a bubble of "Everything is fine. I'm fine." And maybe you are fine.

When you're using drugs, you open yourself up and pull out all those fears or bad moments from your past that you never knew were there. Suddenly those emotions start to rise up and appear in your behavior, but you won't notice it until that moment when you first hit the bottom. That's when you start asking "Why?" and "How did I get to this point?"

So, maybe you tell yourself that instead of using drugs every day, you will use them once a week. Yes. Once a week. That will work.

Ha-ha! Silly goose.

So how do you really break out of this cycle and build a new life? The first thing you need to do and one of the hardest things is to do is *admit that you have a problem.* The second thing is admitting that *you* are the problem. I told you that it was hard!

Now the third thing is letting go.

What do you think is harder—letting go of the drug or letting go of the people you surround yourself with? Especially if those people are those you have known since your first day of school. When you make a conscious decision to break free of the crutch you've been using to get through life, you might think, *Well, if I let them all go, I'll be all alone.*

So. Fucking. What.

If you want to get a different result, you need to do things differently, and that includes overhauling the people you choose to surround yourself with. After all, even if you're surrounded by people, you still can feel very alone. And newsflash: there are other people in the world! You can make new and better friends, friends who support you in your new, positive habits and who won't pull you back down again.

This is what I love so much about consciously manifesting: we attract what we focus on, which was hard for me to understand at first. Why was it so hard? Well, just because I was using drugs to feel good didn't mean everything was bad. I mean, in many ways, I was a good person, helping others more than I was helping yourself. According to the universal laws, that should be a good thing. Working or having your own company, making clients happy, making your partner happy or your boss happy, all of these are positive things, right?

So, how could these negative thoughts and bad things keep happening? How did I still end up with nothing? And when I say nothing, I mean nothing!

I'm going to sum it all up in an easy-to-understand format:

- Happiness is the starting point for real change.
- Self-love is happiness. If you are not happy with yourself, you will always look for other ways to bring yourself happiness.
- Letting go of drugs (or whatever crutch you are relying on) and toxic friends, even the close ones, is necessary if you want to be fulfilled.

- Let go. Accept your past. Understand it. Be aware of how history keeps repeating itself and make a conscious effort to break those patterns of behavior.
- Stop saying "I can't" or "I haven't."
- Face your fears! Identify what's triggering them and work on the root cause. Whether it's a friend/family member, drugs, alcohol, or anything else, *separate* yourself from the things that trigger your fears and those habits that make you act out of fear. Choose instead to have love and happiness in your world.
- Don't start a relationship because of the fear of being alone.
- Choose love over fear. Always.
- Gratitude is one of the most powerful forces for change, and it works instantly!

- Believe in yourself. I like to call it betting on yourself.
- Don't expect anything from anyone besides yourself.
- Meditate.
- Mind your own business; it just doesn't matter what your friends have or do.
- Think positive thoughts.
- They say, "Happy wife, happy life." I say, "Healthy life, happy life."
- Expect and accept miracles.
- *Really* think about what makes you *really* happy.

Exercise

Be brutally honest with yourself. What are the crutches you rely on to get you through life? Maybe it isn't as dramatic as drugs, but are you having a glass of wine every day, kidding yourself it's just a little treat? Or are you a comfort eater? Comfort shopper?

Make a list of all your unhealthy habits, those things you do that you feel guilty about doing and keep telling yourself you're going to stop. One day ...

Now that you have your list, put it somewhere you will see every day. I am not expecting you to be able to stop doing them overnight (although maybe you can, in which case, go you!), but when you feel yourself feeling for that crutch, look at your list and ask yourself *why*? What has been triggered in you that makes you behave that way? What might have happened in your past that you need to let go? If you then still feel the need to rely on your crutch, that's OK. But the first step to releasing those negative patterns of behavior is to identify them so you can then understand them and let them go once and for all.

Don't be afraid to seek professional help with this. There is no shame in getting some support with what can be an incredibly difficult process. A good therapist can help you identify your triggers and help you come up with more positive coping strategies while you work on releasing the underlying cause once and for all.

Ultimately, if you're happy with who you are, the need for those crutches will simply evaporate.

3

When I moved to NYC, I was twenty-eight years old. Before I left, I told myself that I would arrive in NYC, go to the interview my uncle set up for me, and if I didn't get that job, I'd look for something else, even if it meant I might need to wipe tables like I was a teenager.

The interview didn't go well, and I found myself working at the Creperie Spot in West Village.

I got so good at making crepes that I used to be called the crepe man! I was acting like the soup Nazi from Seinfeld. It wasn't long before I was so good at it that the lines for my crepes got longer and longer. I'd start my shift at 5:00 p.m. and not finish my last crepe until 4:00 a.m. On weekends, I used to finish between 5:30 and 6:00 a.m.—last crepe, anyone?

On the weekends, I had a cute blonde girl called Kristen working with me. I think she was from Florida, and she was always so nice and smiley to the customers. No matter how long the line was or how many long hours she worked, she maintained that upbeat attitude—and what did she get for it? Those customers treated her like she owed them something!

One day I got so upset on her behalf, so I asked her, "How do you do it? How the fuck can you smile all day like nothing bothers you? You're not drinking, you're not getting high. *How the fuck can you do that every day?*"

Kristen's reply was simple: "Well, Z, I wake up every morning and decide to be happy. No one can make that decision for me. Some people want to be sad; some want to wake up angry. I decide to be happy, and none of you-all going to change it."

There you go. I was beyond impressed. Kristen was an inspiration to me and one of the reasons I'm where I am today.

I'm going to explain the rules of life that have worked for me. If you follow these rules, I promise you will see results.

What I'm about to share with you is not easy to do, but it *is* 100 percent possible. If I can do it, anyone can. Besides, nothing good comes easily, right?

There is no greater pleasure for me than sharing this with you, knowing that soon you will start to benefit and shine. Now, it took time for me to fully integrate these rules. But I persevered, and over time, my changed habits became a natural part of my routine and a natural part of my way of thinking.

I'm going to caveat this by saying that just because you make these changes doesn't mean you stop being upset or having emotions. The difference will be *how you're going to handle those emotions and how you're going to perceive those bad situations as they arise.*

Are you going to let unpleasant emotions affect the rest of your day, your relationships, work, and experiences? Or will you be able to control those emotions, understand how you got to this point in the first place, and fix it?

My Rules for Living Your Best Life

We all have our ups and downs in life, but when we lack an understanding of why things are happening to us, we'll fight and resist the ups and downs quite strongly, especially the downs. It can be hard to recognize that those downs are the Universe sending us a lesson we need to master before we can move up to the next level of understanding.

Think of life like a computer game where you need to level up before you can face the next set of challenges and enjoy the bigger rewards.

For example, when you work for a company, you are essentially helping your boss become who he wants to be. You put in all that effort, hoping he sees or values your contribution, loyalty, and efforts and gives you what you deserve.

So how do you feel when 98 percent of the time, you get a 1 percent raise—far from what you think you are worth? Unfair, right?

But then fear kicks in. Maybe that 1 percent really is all you're worth. Maybe you don't deserve better. Maybe your help wasn't as valuable as you thought. You think about finding another job, one where you're appreciated, and even more fear washes over you. You question yourself, thinking, *If I quit this job, how long will it take me to get a new one?* Or maybe you fear being uncomfortable: *I get on well with the people at work. Can I have the same connection in a new job?* Or, *Do I really want the hassle of starting all over again?*

These kinds of thoughts can apply to any situation in your life you want to improve. They are the ones that *block* you from being who you could be.

Don't get me wrong; there are lots of people who are OK with staying where they are for little recognition. They are OK with their paycheck, they are OK with paying their house loans, they are OK with paying college loans, they are OK with giving away their money that they work so hard for every day to put food on their table, pay their bills, and pay a high tax rate. They are OK living the way of the system, and that's 100 percent fine, if *you* are 100 percent fine with it! Otherwise, you will be miserable for the rest of your life, hoping your kid will one day break the cycle for you, so you can live through them instead.

Some people try, maybe once or twice. They take a risk, trying desperately to get out of the rat race, and fail. And because of that failure, they decide they prefer the safety of the system. I can understand that.

But I say no to being comfortable and afraid! I say try again, and again, and again, until you get there! Do you think Michael Jordan became who he is because he was good-looking and tall? Do you think Bill Gates or Steve Jobs, or any other hi-tech billionaire just got lucky on their first go? Don't you think all of them needed to work hard and had to motivate themselves to become better? The differences between them and you are as follows:

- They weren't afraid to try again! And again and again!
- They weren't afraid to fail. In fact, they recognized they weren't failures; they were learning opportunities.

- They recognized that setbacks are a part of the journey.
- They weren't afraid of the question "What if?"
- They didn't have in their vocabulary the word *can't*.

Instead, they focused on "how":

- How did this happen?
- How can I improve?
- How do I increase my income?
- How do I stop *xyz* from happening again?

Those are winner questions. They are questions that take the negative and turn it into a positive by learning, adjusting, asking the right questions, and most importantly, betting on themselves! Oops, I shouted, but that was an important one.

Without caring what others may say or think, they just got on with what they needed to do.

Most of us believe that we can't just give up work because we have obligations like rent/food/utilities/kids. So, on top of our fears of failing, if we do what we love, we can sometimes face that fear of *how will I provide for my family?*

Personally, knowing what I do now, I'd be happy quitting my job because I know the Universe will provide for me. But I'm not asking you to quit your job if you're not ready. What I *do* want you to do right now is believe in yourself.

Belief in yourself means you seek only your own approval, instead of constantly seeking it from others. Yes, it will be hard in the beginning. Yes, it will take time. Yes, it may cost you less sleep, TV, and so on, and yes, there will be many sacrifices along the way. But it will be worth it!

For example, let's say you are working at a market, taking any position you can so you can learn the ropes of how to order supplies, where to order, how to find suppliers, how to deal with supply, how to run the tills, how to keep produce fresh, how to be in a good relationship with your suppliers, how to make operations run smoothly, and so on. Then, you look for a way for you to *do the same things yourself*. Maybe offer your employer a deal, asking them to invest in a new location, and you run it on a fifty-fifty basis.

Think outside the box. Think about how you can improve things.

When you start thinking about it, you can always transform fear into something good. Opportunities are there. You just need to recognize them and realize that if you can't see them, it is *you* who is blocking you from seeing them.

Have you ever walked down the street and noticed, say, a car you thought was rare, but once you see it, you start to see a bunch of those cars? It's the same with opportunities; they are out there. They are not rare. Be on the lookout. Start believing in yourself and in your ideas. To love yourself is not a selfish thing. It is the best way to be happy.

Now let me be clear: I'm not recommending you let your ego run riot, then start treating people as if they are below you. That's not what self-love means! Simply love yourself for who you are, and don't obsess over what others think of you or how they look at you, or who is better/more successful.

Let me tell you a story about a very famous man who traveled to Europe. This man was known to be very humble, happy with who he was as a person. Even though he was a very wealthy man, he didn't really care about how he looked or what he was wearing.

As he was walking along the street, a group of people noticed him. They were wearing smart suits and ties, and the famous man was wearing sloppy clothing. One of the guys in the group approached the man and said, "What are you wearing? Aren't you embarrassed, walking like this in the street? A man like you, with your name and wealth, should not walk around looking like that!"

The man looked at the guy, smiled, and replied, "The embarrassed person here is you, my friend, thinking I'm not comfortable with what I'm wearing. Maybe you should look in the mirror and say that to yourself, because it appears you are the one with the problem here."

The point of the story is those who love themselves, really love and value themselves, don't care what anyone thinks of them; they don't need someone's opinion or advice on what they decide to wear or anything else for that matter!

You need to move away from people who are blocking you. Think about *how* they may be blocking you. It can be subtle. Don't make excuses like, "They are my friends/family. They know what's good for me. They have my best interests at heart." But do they even *know your heart*? Do they know what you want, or is it that they know what they want for you—or from you?

There is a big difference there.

Let's start with family. You might not want to block them out. I understand that. They will be there in the good and the bad times, at least in my experience. I had a tough time growing up, as you know, but today I can say my mom and dad played a big role in my life, and all of it is what has made me who I am today. Lovers and friends come and go, but those who stay are usually family.

Have you ever had time to think about and analyze a past relationship? Have you ever noticed that ex-partners actually have similar bad qualities to yours? Did you ever wonder why this keeps happening to you, over and over again? The answer is very simple, and you can probably guess what I'm going to say, but I'm going to say it anyway.

It's because of you!

It's your way of life, your thoughts, your actions. If your life is a mess, most likely you're going to attract the same messed-up people into your life. Think about it. If you are using drugs and drink a lot, would you want someone in your life who is the opposite? A real Goody Two-shoes? No way! You want someone who will enjoy the same things, accept you for who you are and all of your bad habits, go out to parties, blah, blah, blah, blah! You know it's true!

If you keep behaving the same, you will attract the same people. Like attracts like, and all that.

I want you to stop and ask yourself what you are doing wrong that you can change to attract new people into your life who want to go to the same places you want to go, both metaphorically and literally.

For example, if you are going out to places that attract negative behavior, find another way to have fun. In my case, I cut out the nightlife and stopped going to all those lounges, parties, and restaurants I knew would be frequented by people I used to have fun with. It wasn't easy. But it's easier than you think.

I realized I could truly have more fun reading books or going to the gym, riding my bike on the Hudson, being with family, meeting girls at the park or a coffee spot, and appreciating life and what I have. And the bonus: no hangovers!

All of this helped me to attract the right people who are around me today. I cannot express how much it has helped; you'll have to experience it for yourself.

Toxic friends must be removed from your life. I dated a girl once, who kept telling me that cutting people off was a negative thing.

I 100 percent disagree! If people don't appreciate you and hold you back from your dreams (usually due to their own insecurities), they are not good people to have in your life. You have *one* life.

I knew a girl, who I'll just call M, a friend of a friend. M was on and off with a guy, and she made sure my friend knew all about it. M even left her hometown and moved to another state to be close to this guy, and every day it was just drama, drama, drama with those two. On top of all that, she wasn't doing well at work and was struggling with money.

Still, my friend considered M her best friend. Don't get me wrong. When she needed someone to be there for her, M was there. If she needed advice, M was there.

Now let me give you a picture of my relationship with my girlfriend during this time. I'm from New York, doing well. Whatever my girlfriend needed or wanted, she got it. If something happened and she needed me, I was on the first flight to her state to see her. Dream boyfriend, right?

However, whenever we got into an argument, she used to call her best friend for advice, who'd always start by saying,

"Well, when I was in a similar situation, M said ..." Now let me ask you this, and be honest with yourself: If your best friend has the life of her dreams and you don't, how would you advise her? Would you give her sincere advice? Would you be in the space to give 100 percent pure and helpful advice to your best friend?

If you say yes, you're just lying to yourself.

I'll give you another example. You wake up and get into an argument with family, friends, or a boyfriend. You're pretty upset. How will you perform at work? Would you be 100 percent focused? Would you be able to put a real smile on your face? Would your customer service be polite/patient?

- No.
- No.

- And probably no!

So why do you think you would be able to get a sincere answer from your best friend? Just because of their title of best friend?

There is a joke in the army I remember well. Someone tried to join the air force, but when they got rejected, they joined Missiles Against Planes on the basis that if they couldn't fly, they'd shoot down the planes so no one else could either.

If you have what someone else wants, don't look to them for sincerity when you need advice.

If only we could all understand that *we* have the power to change by adjusting our mindset and seeing that we can make a big difference in our lives simply by adjusting how we think about things.

The best advice you will ever get is from your own mind and your own heart. If you really need additional support, go to someone who doesn't have anything to gain from the situation, someone neutral. The best advice I've received has been from people who were at the same stage as me, or who were doing better than me and wanted to see me achieve the same success, people who weren't afraid if I leveled up, they might get left behind.

Before you give someone the title of best friend, they should be able to

- be there for you 95 percent of the time (because they should have their own life too)
- lift you up rather than focusing on the bad
- back you up, even if your idea makes no sense to them or they disagree

- be loyal and honest
- have a healthy mindset and lifestyle
- support you no matter what
- act like your family (or be even closer)

I know a lot of people, but there are only one or two I would call best friends. My best friends are part of my family.

I'll tell you a story. My mom came to visit me in NYC. She had some concerns about her breast, so I told her to get it checked out. I had a feeling something was wrong, but as usual, she ignored my advice.

One day, my brother called me out of the blue. I say out of the blue because, at the time, my brother was not speaking to me because of some money I owed him. I hadn't heard a word from him for three years. At the time, he was living in London, and I was in NYC, so keeping in touch was hard anyway, but he had ignored me for all that time.

When my brother rang, I was with my old boss and his wife. As soon as I saw his name come up on my phone, I told my boss, "Something's happened with my family. Something bad."

My boss asked, "How do you know?"

I told him how we hadn't spoken for three years, so something must have happened to my mom or dad.

Sure enough, when I answered the call, the first thing my brother said was "Mom just got hit by a motorcycle." He went on to say that when she was examined in the hospital, they found out she had cancer. For some reason, my family had been afraid to tell me.

While my mom was in the hospital, my dad—yes, the same man who'd left us—was there every day visiting her. Every day, he'd go straight from work to sit with her along with my mom's sisters, my brothers and sister, my cousins and their kids—you get the picture! My mom was so much loved, but oh how the world stopped when she was injured, and we found out she had cancer.

Support is important, whether from old or new family. But to be able to help others, you need to be able to help yourself.

There is a saying, God helps those who help themselves, and I believe that with all of my heart. As soon as I was OK with myself, as soon as I accepted myself by understanding my past, I was able to forgive myself, which allowed me to move forward. I saw the light when I realized I had all the power I needed to make the first step out from the dark to the light. Simple as that.

To build your dream life, you need to start living it. I know this sounds counterintuitive. We're so used to thinking that we have to wait until we *have* what we want to *be* and *do* what we want. In fact, if we *become* the person we want to be and begin to *do* what we want, we will inevitably *have* what we want—and have a lot more fun along the way!

So, if your dream life is to be rich and give back to your country or family, now's the time to do it. Start by imagining what you will do when you have the amount of money you dream of. My dream is to create shelters for the homeless and provide plenty of food for them. My biggest dream of all is to build affordable housing for everyone and for everyone to be able to renovate their apartment for free so that that all people can live in a decent, happy environment.

This how I started to live my dream:

- I chose one day a week to help the homeless. Every Friday, I go to the market next door to my building, and I buy all the cooked chicken they have, which usually costs between fifty and eighty dollars. I then take the food to Central Park or a place near my area and give it to those who are hungry. I also have a construction company, so while at first, I wasn't able to offer full renovations for free, I could provide extra labor staff for free. I knew it wouldn't make much of a difference to me, but it would definitely make the client smile.

This was how I started living my dream life before I had everything I wanted. I gave what I could without it affecting my happiness.

What do I mean by it not affecting my happiness? Have you ever had the feeling of getting something that you wanted, knowing you don't actually have the money? You felt guilty for making that purchase or regret spending that money when there were more important things you needed.

This is the feeling I want you to overcome. To overcome it, you will need to find a way to be happy with yourself and with what you have, in order to gain more! *Much* more! I want you to be happy and content with the amount of money you have now, whether it's one dollar or a hundred dollars.

Exercise

I want you to take a good, hard look at your life. Who or what is holding you back? Are there any people you need to minimize contact with or cut out completely? Do you have any bad habits you need to eliminate?

It's great to know what you need to remove, but if you don't actively replace them with something you want, you'll find that the Universe has a funny way of sending you things you *don't* want.

Write out what your dream life would look like. Make it as detailed as possible so that you feel as though you're already living it. Then think about how you can make things happen for you right now.

So, for example, if your dream life includes regular days at the spa, look at how you can recreate this more economically at home. Buy posh bath salts, light some candles, have some incense burning. Make it a weekly ritual to relax and unwind. You'll be surprised by how luxurious it can feel. Or contact local spas and see if they have any deals. They may well have regular special offers that you can afford, and you didn't know about it because you assumed you needed more money.

Maybe your dream life includes working with a personal trainer. Find workout videos online (Joe Wicks is a good person to look for) or sign up for an online fitness challenge. There are plenty of free ones. Or maybe you can skill-swap with a personal trainer. Perhaps you know how to build websites, and they need help with theirs. You don't always need money to create your dream life. You can start having the things you want right now if you look for opportunities.

Never say never, because limits are like fears—often just an illusion.

—Michael Jordan

4

Shall we talk about the Michael Jordan effect?

Michael Jordan, the basketball player and actor in *The Last Dance*, had a very particular way of treating his teammates during practice. He'd yell at them and make them feel weak or soft compared to him. Why? Was he being mean for the sake of it? Or did he have a good reason?

Let's face it. As a child, you were probably yelled at by your parents when you did something you shouldn't. I'm not saying it's a good approach, but there's a high chance it came from a place of frustration. While there are better ways of expressing frustration, when your parents did this, you knew it came from wanting you to do your best. You stopped making that mistake because you knew what would happen if you did it again.

Now when someone yells at me, I try to see their point of view. I try to see what positives I can get from the situation. If I've done something wrong, I have the opportunity to change my behavior or apologize. I can also decide that the other person does not have a valid point to make and keep doing what I'm doing. Ultimately, how I react is entirely within my hands. I'm going to keep coming back to this point over and over: you have the power to control how you react to life to choose the best possible way forward.

Michael Jordan treated his teammates like that because he wanted to win! He saw potential and believed in his teammates, so he wanted them to match his level of motivation. He wanted to challenge them, build up their strength. And that's why I love Michael Jordan! Because that's how I see life: those bad moments were really good moments that shaped me to who I am today—fearlessly happy!

It's time to get serious.

I'm going to walk you through some steps I've mentioned before. If you follow them, you will be living your dream life too. What that dream life looks like doesn't matter. What matters is that *you* are happy with it. Not your family, not your friends, not people on the street. No one else!

You'll find yourself proudly singing the Frank Sinatra song "My Way."

Now, speaking of Frank Sinatra, most people know him from his songs or movies. You may even know about his association with the Italian mob. But did you know about the good Frank did in his life? He really is my idol for helping people.

Did you know he was one of the first to stand up for black rights during a time when African Americans weren't even allowed in certain places and areas? When Frank performed a show in Las Vegas, if anyone at the venues made trouble for the African Americans on his crew, he wouldn't perform. He stood up for black rights every chance he had.

Did you know he used to have a private jet company? On those jets, he'd fly flags of the country he was performing for. Why? Who cares about flags? Well, all of the profits from those shows would go to a charity he chose from that country. Given that he could make a few million from his shows, that truly was a lot of money to give away.

Read on if you want to be like Frank and have millions to give away or simply want to make the world a better place, whatever that looks like to you.

Discomfort

The only way to be a better version of you is to get out of your comfort zone. When we talk about our comfort zone, you can take that as a euphemism for being lazy. The reason we stay here is because it's, well, comfortable! We know where we are and where we stand when we stay in this zone, which isn't necessarily a bad thing, but if you want to be a better version of yourself, you need to push yourself to do something that scares you, something you've been avoiding, something you know will be good for you in the long term but might be difficult or even painful right way. I'm not going to sugarcoat it. When you decide to break free of your comfort zone, it's no fun, at least not in the beginning.

For example, if you want to lose weight, you need to start exercising, so you might go to the gym at least three times a week, if not more. You will need to eat less, and you will probably want to change the timing and substance of your meals.

There's nothing stopping you from doing these things right now but the safety and security of your comfort zone. Why go to the gym when you could stay home, put your feet up, and binge-watch Netflix? Why change your eating habits when you could stuff yourself with chocolate cake?

Because that's how you're going to see the results you want! If you want to change your life, you've got to change your thoughts and behaviors. You need to let go of those things that don't serve the you you're becoming.

I understand that it is hard to change all those aspects of yourself that don't fit into your new life. I'm not asking you to make an overnight transformation. You are the one who needs to figure out the best way for you to do it. But you need to start and start now. You simply have to if you want the life you're envisioning.

Pushing toward your goals doesn't mean you have to push yourself too hard. A baby doesn't start to walk as soon as they join the world. Things take time, patience, and practice. How many times do babies fall over? And they usually giggle and stand right up again! All you need is to value yourself and your time and start with those baby steps. But it's amazing how fast you can progress once you get the ball rolling.

Examples of baby steps might be choosing to wake up earlier or go to sleep earlier so you feel refreshed instead of tired all the time. The choice is yours; the time is yours; the motivation comes from you if want to change. The motivation comes from you being able to focus your mind, thoughts, and energy on what is truly best for you, however that looks.

Think about this for a second. When you were a kid and your mom and dad told you not to do something, you usually did the opposite, right? You didn't care what other people did. You did what you thought was best. But for some reason, as we get older, we start to care more and more about what others think and make decisions to please them rather than ourselves. Time to put yourself first again.

I repeat: "The Universe helps those who help themselves." Stop looking for permission, stop waiting to be told what to do. Just make some changes according to how you want to live your life.

What will be the first baby steps you are going to take to step out of your comfort zone? Make a list, buddy!

The Value of Time

When we were at school, all we cared about was when the day would end. We didn't understand or appreciate what the school system was giving us. All we could think of was break times, not being late, school sports, a school sweetheart, our next exam, and so on. We didn't care about the class itself or the value of the education the system was giving us.

But if we look back on those times with advantage of hindsight, we understand what a gift it all was. You see, what we didn't realize was that the system gave us our first glimpse of being responsible and valuing our time.

Aside from facts and figure, school taught us the importance of the following:

- being on time for class
- working to an exam schedule
- doing homework and assignments on time
- being responsible for your actions and your property

If you look back over your school days, I'm sure there are many other valuable things you can find to add to this list, but what I want you to focus on here is the value of *time*.

In the army, that was the first thing I was taught. To show us the value of time, they would give us unrealistic assignments that were impossible to achieve, and it was *incredibly* upsetting. What made it so frustrating was that my commanding officer had only been in the army for three months longer than I had, yet there he was, giving me those stupid timing assignments no one could achieve, at least not as a unit.

For example, they would ask us to run from one point to another point in a few seconds. On top of that, you had to be in formation, and each line had to have three people and be completely even! So, if there were twelve people in the unit, we could have four lines with three people in each line. All fair and reasonable, right? Sure—*if* everyone in my unit was running as fast as I was. But add in the time constraints, and the more you failed, the more time you realized you needed, and you entered a downward spiral.

I hated it, but it certainly taught me to *value time*.

For some reason, we don't value our time, thinking we are going to live forever, so we can put off going after our dreams instead of living in the moment.

Let's discuss why it is so important to value time. Most of us trade our time for money. You are not paid for sleeping. You are not paid when you're not working, say because you're sick or on leave. Think about when you get a job; you can't go to your boss and ask for a raise if you've only been there a week. But after a few years of loyal service, you can ask for a raise for the following reasons:

- You've invested hours into your job.
- You haven't been fired yet, so you must be doing something right!

- It's cheaper to give you a raise than hire a replacement.

If you're asking for a raise, you must value your time, right? But if you're working for someone else, how much you make is determined by how much *they* value your time.

The question is, do you want someone else to value your time, or do you want to do it yourself?

If you are happy where you are, then fine, don't make any changes. But if you feel you deserve more, either from your boss or from yourself, then either go ask for it or find a way to do it yourself. (If you're reading this book, I'm pretty sure you are wanting more and are deserving more.)

This doesn't mean quit your job tomorrow and open your own business but start planning your way out. Keep your eyes peeled for opportunities, plans being cooked up, and work on believing in yourself. Swapping time for money is only *one* way to make money. You can also trade money for money (e.g., investments or bitcoin), and you can trade ideas for money (e.g., write a book and enjoy passive income, making money while you sleep).

I tried asking for a raise when I was working for someone else, and every time I got a no or a small upgrade on my payroll, that just wasn't enough. When I was homeless and sleeping in a company van, I decided to bet on myself. With a bit of help from my parents, I gave my boss one more chance to give me what I wanted and deserved, and when he said no, I made my move. Looking back, he did me a favor. I gained so much more in the long run.

Sacrifice

You can't get to where you want to go if you're not willing to *sacrifice*. I know it's hard, I know it sucks to give up things you love and enjoy, *but this is the only way.* What do I mean by sacrifice?

- Sacrifice going out.
- Sacrifice spending time with people you love.
- Sacrifice being on call for people who don't value your time.
- Sacrifice vacations.
- Sacrifice things that give you instant gratification.

My mom and dad sacrificed their dreams to put food on the table and pay bills in a way that I'm so grateful for. It is hard, though, seeing how my mom is still stuck in the past. I feel it's my fault in a way.

When my mom was pregnant with me, she was at university, studying for her degree. In her final year, her world collapsed, and she had to make a choice. She chose me, my brother, and my sister, dropped out of university, and went to look for a job. She stopped following her dreams and chose responsibility instead.

That is a noble choice to make, but when you sacrifice yourself for others, if it's not what you truly want to do, you may begin to blame yourself for those decisions and not be able to see the good that came from that sacrifice.

With the support of my mom and me, my older brother became a lawyer. He's doing well for himself, his wife, and two kids. My other brother is an IT guy. He has a girlfriend and two kids and is very happy with what he has. My sister has six kids! And somehow, she manages to juggle her children with a happy marriage.

Looking at that, you could say my family's pretty successful. My mom's grandchildren give her so much joy, but for some reason, it's not enough, and I feel it is because of the choices she made earlier in her life.

Maybe if she'd sacrificed time with us when we were little, she'd be happier with her life now. You shouldn't be afraid to sacrifice. Look at athletes who travel all year long, away from their families, to give them a better life. Or people who work months in the mines, to provide their children with the best they can. As long as you make healthy choices and show your children the value of hard work and going for your dreams, they will understand.

Of course, I'm not saying abandon your kids! Children need love, attention, and time. But some short-term sacrifices made with love and understanding will be OK. Let's be honest: it doesn't matter what you do. You're going to make mistakes as a parent, and children don't fully understand their parents' decisions when they're young. You are showing them how to fight for their dreams, which is such a gift.

Going back to Michael Jordan, he and all the other truly great players sacrificed family time for the love of the game and their dream because of their winner mentality and wanting to be the best.

In the NBA bubble, LeBron mentioned how he sacrificed his sixteen-year-old kid's birthday to play for the club and the fans. Think how *big* a sacrifice that is. But now LeBron James is at a point where he doesn't need to make any more money. He can retire, not work another day, and be with this family full-time. Do you think his kid was mad at him for not being there for his birthday? Probably. But let's look at the big picture. Does he now have everything he wants and needs? Does he get whatever birthday celebration he wants and more? Does he know his dad loves him? Of course! *And* King James got what he was working for. Nothing can ever take away from him the fact that he was the NBA champ.

I think you see my point. Sacrificing for a good and healthy reason is a *good* thing. You will make yourself *and those around you* happy! Happiness is contagious and will spread to your whole family.

However, you will not be rich if you can't feel rich with what you have right now, in the present.

To reach your lofty dreams, you need to feel good with what you have *now*.

Whatever you have now should make you feel like the richest person in the whole world. You are as rich as a billionaire, even if you have only one dollar, not because you can spend money like one but because you are happy with what you have *now*. The money will naturally follow.

You might even find that the billionaire thinks you have more than they do just because of your happiness, your love of life, the love *in* your life, and your approach to life!

Start focusing on what you *do* have, instead of focusing on what you don't have. If you find yourself dwelling on what you don't have, start to practice gratitude and say, "I'm thankful for ..." List at least three things you can be grateful for right now, even if it's just the sun in the sky, the sound of birds in the trees, or the smell of a rose. It'll make a positive change in your day—guaranteed!

Gratitude has the power to instantly bring in happier thoughts, which push out the bad ones. Again, slowly, slowly, you will see a shift in your life.

Remember: the quality of your life depends on the quality of your questions. Life is always reflecting back to you what you believe. If you believe that life is hard, then life *will* be hard. When you shift your thoughts toward believing life is fun, easy, or happy, that is what you get back. You won't see a result overnight, but you'll be surprised by just how quickly it does take effect.

Exercises

Discomfort

Think about the life you want to be living. What baby steps can you take *right now* to enjoy that life before you manifest all your dreams, even if it means getting out of your comfort zone?

If you want a slim, healthy body, can you get off the bus or train a stop early? Take the stairs instead of the elevator? If you want to find the partner of your dreams, can you think about the interests you have in common and start doing more of those? If you want to follow a particular career path, do you need to get any qualifications? Can you network with people who are doing what you want to do?

Time

Write out your typical schedule (or maybe even do two, one for a workday and one for your days off). How are you spending your time? How much time are you spending on social media, playing silly games, or watching TV? How much of that time can you divert to creating your dream life?

What baby steps can you take to value your time more? Can you download an app to limit your time on social media? Can you read a book related to your dream life instead of watching a TV show? Can you do one thing a day that supports your goals?

How much time can you free up if you stop doing those things that do not serve your dreams?

Sacrifice

What do you think you will have to sacrifice in order to manifest your dream life?

Make a list of what you think you will have to give up. Then write out the worst- and best-case scenario for what will happen if you do not make those changes and if you do.

Just how far are you willing to go to make sure you get what you desire?

Gratitude

Gratitude is the fastest way to raise your vibration so you can attract the life of your dreams.

I like to repeat this affirmation daily and suggest you do the same:

Thank you.
Thank you for this day.
Thank you for the air I breathe.
Thank you for the gift of life.
I accept and expect miracles.

I say it every morning as soon as I wake up. Then I add to it what I'm thankful for that day. It might be:

- my parents
- family
- the roof over my head
- food on my table
- all of my blessings
- all of my lessons
- my past
- my growth
- attracting new people into my life
- new and old love
- those who I've lost

- all the opportunities I have now and those to come
- my ability to give
- my dog
- my ability to trust
- self-love
- my awesome and loving relationship
- morning sky and sunshine
- nature
- the ability to forgive myself and those who let me down
- the ability to let *go*
- all that is

Every day, you should make a list of things you feel grateful for. Have at least three items on it but make it as long as you like. There is no limit to gratitude!

I suggest including on your list

- your past,

- all of your lessons, and
- growth (self-growth, monetary growth, whatever it is).

As you create your list, really *feel* the emotion of gratitude. After twenty-one days of doing this, you will see a change.

You can also use gratitude to lift your mood. If you feel you are having a bad moment, shift to gratitude as soon as you realize it occurring and say, "Thank you, thank you for this day." This will automatically shift things back to the light, out of the dark, and you will feel better.

Remember, focusing on the good when things are bad is the key to this life shift toward success. When you are thankful for what you have and what is coming, it helps speed up the manifesting.

5

In my last few relationships, I had the same issue: the girl I was dating was with me because she was afraid of being alone. I wasn't exactly in a good place myself, so neither of us was in a good position to start a healthy relationship. Still, I was having fun, and she was looking for the same thing; we just never seemed to dig into the real reason we liked each other. We only discussed the problems with our exes and never talked about our own problems. We blamed our exes for *everything* while forgetting a few important things:

1. No one forced us to be with that person. We could have left as soon as we noticed the issues.

2. We never stopped and asked ourselves why we were attracting the same kind of people into our lives over and over again.

3. We didn't consider whether it was really our ex who had the problem or whether the truth lay closer to home.

Now, I'm not saying that what you think about your ex isn't true. I'm not saying that they didn't have problems. What I am saying is the way you dealt with it was the real issue. Staying when you could have left, even if after giving them two or three more chances. Being blinded by love and hoping that things would get better even though your heart told you it wouldn't.

Staying because you don't think you could find someone better.

I'm telling you right now, yes, you will. Once you make a conscious decision to build a better life for yourself, you'll start attracting better people. The Universe sends along those who can help you get to where you want to be, including the perfect love when you are ready.

When you stop making fear-based decisions, you'll be able to see how many options you really have. There's so much your fear stops you from seeing. We attract our partners from our feelings, so if you are at a point in life where you are happy, then a better boyfriend or girlfriend will come along. By contrast, if you still think everything is bad, full of drama, or steeped in fear, then you will continue this cycle in your relationships.

Don't get me wrong. Life isn't all flowers and rainbows. That's the nature of human existence. Even if you're in a happy place in your life, there will always be ups and downs. But the way you handle those downtimes will be much easier when you tackle them with love and happiness instead of from fear and drama.

Let's look at the Kardashians for a second. I bet you've seen at least one episode of their show. The reason it went on for so many seasons is because we all feel connected to their situations, even though we don't have the same bank balance, especially when it comes to dealing with relationships.

Take Khloe, for example. I love her so much because of how she changed her life to achieve her goals, which at the time were weight loss and wanting to have a baby. From an early age, we all saw her struggles with those issues. As the show progressed, you could see how she shifted her mindset and took responsibility for her life, knowing she was the only person who could do so.

In order to lose weight, she made some simple changes:

- Go to the gym daily.
- Maintain a healthy diet.
- Focus on a healthy life and break free from unhealthy habits from her youth.

It was a little harder to make the right changes when it came to having a baby. We all watched her struggle to find the right man despite her beauty. But once she started to believe in herself, she attracted the right people, where before she was attracting all the wrong people who just wanted a piece of her and her family.

I feel Khloe made her earlier choices out of fear. Looking at her today, I don't think fear is an issue for her anymore. She looks amazing! She has kids and a loving and supportive family.

Choose Love over Fear

Choosing love is not a weakness. Choosing love does not make you stupid or naïve. Choosing love means choosing to see the good in the bad of any situation in life. It's understanding the issue and asking yourself what you can do better to overcome it.

This includes health issues, which usually come from bad habits, stress, or working too hard. Think of the intense lives of athletes. The reason why athletes are able to recover from their injuries is because they take care of themselves and their bodies, understanding that if they want to perform at their peak, they have no choice. They approach their issues with love and nourishment, which makes recovery easier.

On the same note, those who love their sport less or stop loving the game tend not to gradually lose their way. The pressure of major injuries or repeated minor injuries can leave the athlete unable to recover, needing to leave the game.

I'll give you two examples:

- Kobe Bryant loved his sport so much that he kept fighting his injuries over and over again. As soon as he stopped loving it, he left the game and looked for his next move.

- Andrew Luck (NFL quarterback) had no luck when it came to injuries, but when the love of the game was in him, he was able to overcome his injuries until he gave up. In his last interview, he admitted that he loved the game, but the passion for it was no longer in him.

"If you're afraid to fail, then you're probably going to fail" (KB Rip).

As I mentioned earlier, during my time working at the creperie in West Village, I met an amazing young woman, Roni. She is everything I want in a woman—no joke! I met her when she was twenty years old, and I was twenty-eight. As I said, I didn't like working at the creperie, but looking back now, I can see it was actually pretty good fun. I met a lot of decent people, some of whom I'm still in touch with.

But at the time, I felt used, underpaid, and lost. When I met Roni, she ... *wow*. Just writing about her gives me a warm, loving feeling. Roni is the kind of girl who lights up the room just by being there.

Now you're probably asking yourself, *Why is Roni so important?* What does she have to do with me trying to get my life together? When I met Roni, she had already fought cancer three times. She'd been through three chemotherapy treatments and yet was acting like everything was just fine. Her cancer came back a few months after I met her, and her boyfriend had to carry her because she couldn't walk. One time she came in with a wheelchair, but despite all her struggles, she never let it get her down. In fact, I believe that the only reason she was able to overcome her cancer was her approach of love and happiness.

She is a real inspiration to me.

Think about it. You have two choices when it comes to dealing with life's issues:

- Face it.
- Don't face it.

That's it! If you decide to face it, you also have two choices:

- Face it with doubt and fear.
- Face it with love and positivity.

Whichever approach you take, you can't know the outcome. But isn't it easier to choose love? At least you can smile, and you might even make others smile with you. You might not be facing a problem with your health, but the principle's the same. Look at Roni choosing to laugh and focus on the good side of life. If she can do that despite numerous fights with cancer, how small do your problems look in comparison?

It's not that hard to maintain a positive outlook when you get used to focusing on love and finding the silver lining in any cloud, but it does take practice. I know. I was there. When I started to choose love, even when I didn't have any proof of how much difference it could make, I immediately started to see small changes—really small! But a mighty oak tree grows from a tiny acorn. You won't see any changes if you choose fear! Why? Because fear will always block you.

The idea for writing this book came from a desire to help. I know there are already many good books about the law of attraction, but I wanted to share my story because it's so much easier to follow the advice when you know it's genuinely worked for someone.

All of these books share the same concepts and beliefs of how to program your mind to see significant changes, such as the following:

- Choose love over fear.
- Face fear and overcome it.
- Use powerful words to reprogram your thinking.
- Change your habits.

All of those things are important, and as soon as you do them, whether you take my approach or that outlined in any of those other books, change *will* happen. But what then? What happens after you get what you want in life? You need to *maintain* it.

As you can probably tell by now, I love sports, particularly basketball and soccer.

Why? I love the mindset of the players that enables them to win at all costs—MJ, Kobe, and so on.

By the way, being a Knicks fan as a kid, I used to *hate* those players. Where I'm from, everyone loves the Bulls or LA, and as a kid, I always had to be different! I was also the kind of kid people loved to hate because 98 percent of the time I would find a way to either win or get away from a situation. I didn't need to do much to get good grades, but I only got good grades if you challenged me. If I didn't see a challenge, I wouldn't bother.

As a young kid, I was very short, so playing basketball wasn't really an option. The coach used to pass on me, and the dads had even more say in deciding who was going to play, more than the coach. Despite the fact I wasn't going to be a famous basketball player, it never stopped me from showing I could still be the best.

I was always kind of quick, so being the first to get to the basket wasn't my problem. It was the people I was playing who were over six feet tall and could easily block my shot!

I needed to find another way—and I did! I worked on my three points shots. I got so good in any position that whoever I was up against had to stay close; otherwise—boom! I win!

Mind you, despite all my great shots, I can look back and see that I was doing it for the wrong reason. You see, the drive of being the best shouldn't come because you want to do better than your neighbor, your brother, your best friend. It's to do better for *you*. To make *you* feel better, even if you're not the best in the world.

If someone is better than you, maybe it's because they want it more than you, not because they are actually better than you. It's all in your head. If you are coming to work with the mentality of *I hate my job, I don't want to be here,* then it's going to feel like it all day long—and the day will be long! It's the same with sports; if you feel like you don't have a chance of winning, it's going to be incredibly difficult, if not impossible, to win. This isn't rocket science!

If you lost a deal, lost a job, or lost a business, the onus is on you to learn from the experience. Maybe you didn't give 100 percent, you didn't do it from a place of love, or you didn't believe you could make it. I can give you so many reasons why ultimately it was because of you and your mindset, just so you understand that no one is better than you unless you give up

127

on yourself. (And even then, they're not better; they just have a better mindset.)

Whatever you choose to do, stop caring about how anyone else is doing. Stay in your lane! You might think you're competing against them, but you're really only competing against yourself, *to be a better you.*

To summarize,

- If you want to *win*, you need to do what you didn't do yesterday.
- If you want to *win*, you need to get out of your comfort zone.
- If you want to *win*, you need to make the feeling of sacrifice natural, so you don't feel like you're losing out or giving up on something important. If you are doing something you want to do, it shouldn't feel like such a sacrifice.

- If you want to *win*, you need to feel the urge to win so badly that no one—not your family, not your friends, not anyone—can deter you. No one! You are the one driving the car of your life. No one else.

You have to *want* to change your life, really want it, not just pay lip service to the idea. Otherwise, nothing you do will make a blind bit of difference.

It might have taken me a while to get here, but now I can honestly say that I believe in myself. I don't let anything stand in my way or set me back. I mix things up as soon as I feel myself standing still or even going backward (although I don't really go backward these days). I push myself to take action every time I feel I want to stay in bed and do nothing, yet I'm working far less than I used to. I have more time as well because I choose to make the most of every moment and have actively chosen a career that enables me to have more time for my charitable endeavors. I say this because by the time you are reading this book, I will be in a place where I will be even closer to my dream life. I will be building affordable housing. I will have a nonprofit organization to feed the homeless. I will be supplying equipment for kids in schools, as well as scholarships, or maybe even be building a free school.

My dream is bigger than I am, and it will always be like that. I will make it happen with time because I believe that I will with every essence of my being.

Exercise

In order to be able to accept love in all its forms, you first need to be able to love yourself. Start this process by writing a love letter to yourself. In this letter, you should identify the eight (yes, eight!) qualities you love most about yourself. Then describe all the ways in which those qualities have helped you. Close by writing out all the ways in which you can honor these aspects of yourself.

Make this a weekly task and watch how much you can appreciate all the wonderful ways in which you make this world a better place just by being you. Put your weekly letter up somewhere you can read it every day to remind yourself how awesome you are. After you've read it, repeat to yourself, "I am worthy. I am enough."

6

We've covered the fact that if you want to manifest your dream life, you're going to you need to put in the work, but at the same time, you need to balance the amount of work you are doing with relaxing and letting the Universe take the reins. Let it surprise you with what's going to happen. The Universe usually knows far better than we do what is our best way forward and can create a life even better than the one you've imagined.

Remember, you can only control the now and your reaction to it. You can't control every aspect of your environment. You can't control others. You can't control what happens to you. You need to focus on you, the only part of the equation you *can* control. What can you do right now to make your life better? If there's nothing else available, you can always change your mindset.

We tend to stop believing our dreams are possible when we want something so much and work so hard to get it, yet it's just not happening. It's one of the trickiest aspects of manifestation to conquer. You know you need to do the work, but the more work you do, the further away your dreams seem. It's so frustrating.

I'm going to tell you a secret: the reason your dream life isn't here already is because you are trying too hard. All this effort is resulting in frustration, and that frustration is taking your attention away from where it should be. You are focused on the fact that you don't have your dream life yet instead of simply living your dreams, which sends out a signal to the Universe that you're not ready, so it continues to delay.

I know people hate it when someone says to them, "You just need to relax!" And I don't want to be *that* guy, but really, you need to relax and let the Universe lead the way.

Look at it this way: when you go to the gym or start a diet, you know you're not going to see results the next day. It will take between three and four weeks to see any kind of change, and that's only the start of a shift in the right direction.

It's the same with the law of attraction and belief. You put in the work and let your body, mind, and spirit adjust to the changes. Some of us see changes quickly. Others take more time. It's not a race. Remember, you shouldn't be comparing yourself to anyone.

If you keep up with your diet and exercise regime, you *will* see results. If you push yourself too much, you're going to stress your body and cause an injury. It's all about balance. It's the same with manifesting your dreams. If you try to push too fast, it will never happen.

To sum up, the simple way to manifest is this:

- You put in the work.
- Believe it will work.
- Be happy with what you have.
- Let the Universe do the rest.

In time, it will happen. It's universal law. The sooner you let go of fear or imposing a timeline for when it is going to happen, the sooner things will work out for you. It's that easy and that hard.

When we want to manifest something in our lives, we tend to jump all over the place. You can't multitask manifesting! If you want to be a lawyer, you're not going to study to be a doctor, even if you'd like to have a degree in medicine too one day. You go to law school, finish, then move on to study to be a doctor.

You know the saying *you can't have your cake and eat it too*. Prioritize your manifestation list. If love is what you are seeking most of all, then focus on that. If it's a better job or opening a business or having more money, focus on that. When things start to go your way, then you can move on to the next thing that you are looking to manifest.

And remember to be grateful for every little thing that happens to you. Gratitude is the awesome sauce that lubricates the manifestation wheels.

I had this exact issue until I realized that things slowed right down when I was focusing on two things at the same time. I was focusing on manifesting my dream business, but at the same time, I was also looking for love. Eventually, these dreams both came true, but think about how much faster I could have had what I wanted if I'd focused my energies in one direction.

In the end, I chose to pay attention to my business, knowing that if I were to do well there, I would be able to move confidently forward with my life, be there for my family and for my mom and dad. I'd be able to give more and help others in need of food or kids who need items for school. I would be able to build my foundation for a better future for myself and others, not to mention my new love, so that's what I decided I should focus on first.

Let's try a thought experiment. Ask yourself: how would I feel if I had whatever I desire right now? Focus on that feeling. As you focus on that feeling, see if you can note any negative feelings that arise. Fear? Doubt? Mistrust? Those feelings are what's blocking you from the good feeling of having what you want.

We often don't like change or having to adjust to new situations, even if the change is a good thing, like starting a new job that you want. We always have mixed emotions that come with change, like "Yay new job! Go me!" while at the same time that feeling of starting all over again makes us nervous. "Will the staff like me? Will I get along with people? Will they be happy with my work?" All of those mixed emotions are the reason things can be slow to start/change. You need to work on minimizing the negative so the positive can shine through. (It's natural to have *some* negative emotions, and these won't stop your manifestations as long as you are more positive overall.)

If you're finding it hard to let go of your negative self-talk, hear me out. Why even *start* with those thoughts in the beginning? You got *hired*, right? You got hired by being you, didn't you? So, continue being *you*, and you'll be just fine. Do the work you were hired for, add a dash of your innate awesomeness, and you'll be more than fine.

If you notice that things are not working as they should and your manifestations aren't naturally flowing toward you, it means you are overwhelming yourself with negative thoughts that are blocking and delaying you from manifesting your future. *You* are the only reason why things aren't working. Instead of asking,

"Why isn't it working?" and deciding that manifestation is a waste of time, ask yourself, "How are the many ways in which it can work? What do I need to stop doing to make it work? What changes do I need to put into place?" You and only you can understand what your problem/blockages are. I can't do this for you! I can tell you that there is something blocking you; it's not *someone* or *something*. It's you! Fear! Doubt! Overthinking! It could even simply be you deciding that you must be blocked because you don't have what you want, and that thought by itself creates a block!

You might not be able to change the past, but you can most definitely change your future, starting right now.

Shift the Energy of a Bad Day with Your Favorite Song

When you first start down the path toward positive manifestation, it can be hard to make a shift of emotions when you're suddenly faced with things going downhill. First of all, I want you to know that you do not have to feel happy all the time. We are still human after all, and we experience the full range of human emotions, even if our minds are set on being filled with happy thoughts and energy.

When I'm struggling, I use a song that boosts my energy and helps bring me back to a positive outlook. Sure, music won't enable me to forget my problems or make them go away, but it sure does help shift the vibe of my day or at least stop me from overthinking.

Music is very powerful when it comes to lifting your mood. It makes you feel automatically better; you may even want to start dancing or singing along, changing that feeling of stress to one of fun, at least in that moment.

What do I listen to when I need a pick-me-up? My go-to is Bob Sinclair's "Children of the Sky." It's an old song, but it always does the trick!

Find *your* song, a song that never fails to put you in a good mood, whether it's because it has happy lyrics, an upbeat tune, or brings back positive memories. Play it every time you are having a bad day, feel overwhelmed by negative thoughts, or are overthinking life. Even better, put together an uplifting playlist and enjoy a cheerful soundtrack to your life. Put the music on, let go of those thoughts that do not serve you, and trust in the Universe to do the rest.

Remember, love, happiness, and gratitude are the keys for your dreams to come true, so use music to bring you back to those high-vibe emotions.

You need to trust the process in order for it to work. When I say trust, I mean 100 percent trust, guys! If you trust 90 percent and doubt 10 percent, then you will experience a delay of 10 percent. If you trust 60 percent in the process, then you'll have a 40 percent delay until you reach your dream. (And that's if you're lucky. Some people find that if they question the process, that questioning keeps them from their results indefinitely.)

Let me make something super clear here. I started the early chapters of this book by talking about my life and experiences. Often, we focus on the bad side of our past. We tend to blame ourselves or our parents for how we turned out. It's a natural instinct.

But ask yourself this: has focusing on the bad and finding blame helped you in any way? I mean, I can go on and on about my messed-up life, but instead I choose to focus on how my bad experiences shaped me into who I am today and the good that's come out of it. For example:

- My mom chose to let my dad come back home despite how he treated us. This is the bad side of the story. I choose to look at it differently. I choose to see my mom's persistence at not giving up on something she thought was a good thing. It showed me how to keep going against all odds. Even when everyone else stops believing in you, keep going. In the end, my mom got what she wanted.

Was it a good choice? Who can say? At the time, she thought it was, and people do try their best with what information they have at the time, even if to the rest of us it might seem like a crazy decision.

- My dad, with all of his bad choices, kept working like crazy, showing up to work, knowing he needed to keep going, that he needed to put food on the table. Again, I choose to see the persistence of my dad working at his job day after day, and in the end, it paid off for him. He found peace of mind and a secure job where he worked for eighteen years until he was too old to go on. That job gave him stability, gave him his smile back, paid his debts, and most importantly gave him back *me* and his kids believing in him. My dad is proof that there *are* happy endings. Possibilities are available to you every day. You need to see them, then catch them like precious gems and use them to be better.

When things are bad in life, it's like a rainy day. You can focus on the rain, but a break in the clouds gives you a glimpse of how your life could be, that moment of happiness when it's not raining. Don't you want to step out from behind the cloud? From behind the clouds of bad thoughts? Don't you want to see the sun? You might even see a rainbow!

You can choose to have sunny days and rainbows for the rest of your life. When you choose love over fear, that's when the rain will stop.

Exercise

When you start feeling doubt, negative self-talk, or pessimism creeping in, you need to shift your perspective. Put together a play list with songs that put a smile on your face and play it on shuffle so that you have no idea what song will be coming next, but you know you'll love it. Each song should be one that makes you want to fist-pump the air and cry, "Yes! This song is awesome!"

Ideally, dance like no one's watching while you sing along to the song, but if you're not in a position to do that, simply closing your eyes and getting lost in the music for a few minutes will do wonders to lift your mood.

Whatever problem you're currently facing is transient. All things will pass, including this.

Another way to lift your mood is to make a list of all the times the Universe has been there for you. Maybe it brought a person into your life who's made a huge difference to you. Maybe you had a sudden windfall. Maybe you achieved something you thought was impossible. Try to have at least five things on your list, but if you can think of only one thing, that's OK.

Once you've made your list, spend thirty to ninety seconds feeling nothing but pure gratitude for each item on it. Remember, the Universe gave you those people, experiences, and gifts. It has more in store for you, and the more grateful you feel for all the blessings you've received so far, the more blessings you'll see all around you.

7

I think it's time for another story.

Two homeless men were traveling together. One was Jewish, and the other was German. It was close to the Passover holiday, and the Jewish man was telling the German man how amazing this holiday was. The family got together, enjoyed a big meal, and sang songs.

Passover sounded so exciting. The German homeless man decided he wanted to experience this special holiday for himself. He put all his efforts into looking for a family to invite him to join their Passover celebrations, and eventually he found one.

When the day arrived for him to celebrate Passover with the family, he was particularly looking forward to the dinner, since a good meal was hard to come by on the streets. He sat down at the table with his host family as first they blessed the wine and then the romaine deep with salty water. Next came the blessing of the potato, and again the deep with salty waters.

The German didn't understand what was going on. In his head, he wondered, *Where was all the food the Jew had told him about?*

The German was asked to go and wash his hands before the meal. When he returned, he was served matza (a type of flatbread) and *haroset* (a traditional Passover dish made with apples, wine, cinnamon, and walnuts). The German was so disappointed he left without touching his meal and went back to the streets.

A few hours later, he came across the Jewish man. The Jewish man asked him, "How was the dinner?"

The German launched into a torrent of complaints about how terrible the dinner was, before accusing the Jew of lying to him about this amazing holiday. The German was yelling so much it was almost impossible for the Jew to say anything, but eventually he stopped to take a breath, at which point the Jew told him, "If only you had waited for one more blessing, you would have eaten like a king!"

The point of this story is that we all have times when we want to cry about our past, how close we were to our goals and how things blew up in our faces. We have all been in the homeless German man's shoes, where we had an opportunity, but then something happened, and this opportunity slipped through our fingers.

- If only Adam and Eve could have waited until sunset to eat the apple, they would have been spared.
- If only *you* were able to start that diet and stick to it during the first week when it's really tough, you would have lost the weight.
- If only you were able to find time to go to the gym to get a healthy, toned body.
- If only you weren't blinded by love and saw the warning signs that your partner was cheating on you.
- If only you were able to let go when you knew something was wrong.

So let me explain how I see it. Just because something is hard, or things go badly for a bit, doesn't mean it can't still be good for you in some way. It doesn't mean you are on the wrong track and should give up.

If you are smart enough, you will take each situation as a lesson, understanding that life is hard at times, and that is just a part of being alive. But if you are working toward your goals, you get a feeling of joy and happiness at the same time something is bothering you.

Sometimes happiness can be tricky. I get that. You think you're on the right track, but you don't see the signs that are right in front of you showing you what needs to be changed so the wave you're riding won't fade away. You *are* on the right track, but instead of being humble about it, the ego kicks in. Fear and ignorance mix with happiness (which I call fake happiness) and blindside you. The German in the story was so focused on the food or how good the food would be he lost sight of the following:

- the fact that he got invited
- the fact he was with company and out of his normal, unhappy routine
- the fact that he'd been given an opportunity
- the fact he was around good family vibes
- the fact the Universe was there for him
- the fact he was eating

If he had been grateful for all of that, the German would have stayed in the moment, enjoyed everything the Universe was giving him, and then he would have been there for the real feast and enjoyed the best meal of his life.

The Passover blessings that so bored the German are part of the gratitude that Jews show to G–D for being there for them as they bless their way to the good meal.

I see this story as being a metaphor for life; those small steps leading to the big meal are the small steps you should take in order to start living the life of your dreams. There is a good book about mastering Zen called *One Small Step Can Change Your Life* by Robert Maurer. I really recommend you read it because it goes into this process in great depth. If you look at your struggles as a learning experience and not something to give all your attention to, your mindset will help you to see the good in the bad.

Let's say that you have decided that tomorrow you are going to make your first move toward your dream life. You take your bike and start to ride in the direction of your dreams.

Would you prefer to ride on a flat surface for the rest of your life? It might seem tempting, easy even, but think about it. If you were cycling along a path that never changed, would you be able to see any change or progress? Of course not. You need to ride a hill.

Riding a hill might be challenging, but when you reach the top, you'll enjoy an incredible view and have the best time going back down. Maybe you'd like to keep going up because you like working, or maybe you'd like to get up there just so you can have a smooth, downhill ride for the rest of your life. Either way, you need to get past that hill!

Bad can be good if you're able to focus on your end game. If you can learn from your mistakes, facing them should be easier, so don't be afraid of making mistakes.

Instead of fearing what will happen if you fail again, why not think of what would happen if you succeeded?

For example:

- What would I love about being in a great relationship? How would I feel?
- What would happen if I got rich beyond my wildest imaginings? How would I help my family or others who are struggling? How could I bring joy to others?
- What would it be like to live in your dream home and wake up to amazing views from your bedroom window every morning?

What's stopping you from focusing on how you'd feel if you had everything you wanted? If you think reality is what's getting in the way, I'd ask you this:

- Does reality tell you what to wear when you wake up?
- Does reality tell you what you should eat or drink during the day?
- Does reality stop you from doing what you want/need to do?
- Or is it *you* who is controlling your reality?

Your reality is for *you* to control, not the other way round. You will never find out whether you are making the right or wrong choices until you make them, but that discovery is what makes life so fascinating.

Failing is not something we dream about. It is not anyone's goal, but for some reason, we hold onto it and give it our attention. We obsess over our regrets and pain, kidding ourselves that doing this will free us from making another mistake.

Instead of worrying about your failures, tell the Universe with a smile, "You got me this time, but let's see if you get me the next time," Say, "Le Haim" to your failures (which means "For Life" and is a little like saying, "Cheers") instead of feeling miserable for the rest of your life, hoping that eventually that sadness will go away.

Well, I hate to break it to you, but it won't go away if you're stuck in a cycle of bad thoughts or feelings without trying to change your reality. How can you possibly heal if you keep being negative? Even if you decide to run away from the truth, the truth will not run from you.

That's why admitting you made some wrong choices and facing your failures is the beginning of real change. Your fear of failure fades away easily when you are looking forward, not back. You'll be too busy making positive changes to be dwelling on a useless place.

I'll be honest with you. I still have those moments when past failures pop up to haunt me. I know it's no fun when that happens. But now I choose to thank those thoughts for reminding me I'm human, and I tell them that I'm making changes and choosing love instead. I control my thoughts by repeating in my head what I'm grateful for, or I meditate to shift my mood.

This sounds awesome! Sign me up! But how do I start?

For this process to work, you need to really want it but without feeling desperate to have it or imposing a schedule or timeline for when you want to live your dream life. You have to come to it with no expectations and with a mindset that you might have to sacrifice a lot along the way.

I've mentioned that there are a number of steps and suggested meditation as a starting point. Many people like to combine yoga and meditation to help them achieve their dreams, which can be a good starting point. Personally, I tried yoga and didn't really connect to it, but meditation? That was a completely different story.

There are many good mantras I use while meditating. Each one has a unique flavor. When I started to meditate, it took me a while to get into it, which is totally normal. Start slowly and build up; just a few minutes a day can make a big difference, and you will be surprised by how quickly you'll be able to sit for ten, twenty minutes or more.

I started with a simple *om* meditation, just repeating it over and over, flowing naturally with my breath. The whole idea of any kind of meditation is to clear your mind from any distractions. Easier said than done! But it gets easier. Trust me here.

I realized that the best time for me to start meditating was as soon as I wake up, before my thoughts start pouring in, and I'd recommend you try making meditating the first thing you do every day. If you look at your phone and see messages waiting, ignore, ignore, ignore. It's time the world got the message—it's *me*-time first! They can wait. But can your mental state?

Once you feel comfortable with an om meditation, switch it to a morning guided meditation. Try searching for Mary Kate. She has a very good morning meditation that works with gratitude, as well as many other powerful ones. Go onto YouTube and search for meditation. You'll find plenty of free meditations from beginner to advanced.

As soon as I got the hang of it, I was meditating every chance I got! I'd say to myself, "The problem will still be there when you come out of the meditation. That's a fact. But the key here is, do you want to solve the problem with good, calm energy? Or do you want to try to solve your problem with negative, stressed energy?" The answer seemed pretty obvious to me.

These days, I meditate as soon as I get up, during the day whenever I feel I need to, and before ending my night. I even do a sleep meditation as well. I find the morning and while-you-sleep meditations to be particularly powerful. One is programming your subconscious while you sleep, while the other is preparing your day for miracles.

Again, it took me some time to get into this. Why? Because I wasn't able to control my thoughts, which left me frustrated. So, I took it slow and started with a two-minute om. Then those two minutes became five minutes, and before I knew it, I was doing a whole fifteen-minute om meditation. So, be patient with yourself. Give it a chance. If you are able to master your mind and your thoughts,

- You will be able to separate your good from your bad thoughts.
- You will be able to manifest your dream life faster.
- You will be able to separate yourself from those who are holding you back.
- You will be able to see clearly who is your friend and who is not.

- You will be able to make better choices and handle life with a more open mind.
- You will be able to see the opportunity in the obstacle.
- You will be able to handle loss or failure more easily by understanding that it's OK to fail as long as you understand the process of adjusting so that it doesn't happen again.

Another powerful meditation mantra that helps you to recognize your bad thoughts is "Ek Ong Kar Sat Gur Prasad." This meditation will blow your mind—seriously! Look up "2 ½ hour-long Ek Ong Kar Meditation." If you are able to get into this one with a clear mind, you can get high simply with the vibration of the mantra. The feeling after this meditation is unbelievable!

Exercise

This guided meditation script can help shift you from feeling negative to a state of gratitude. You might like to get a friend to guide you through it (in which case, return the favor for them), or you could simply make a recording of yourself reading it so you can relax and enjoy the meditation without worrying about what comes next.

Make yourself comfortable somewhere you know you will not be disturbed. Switch off your phone and any other distractions and settle down. This is *your* time to enjoy. You deserve this.

Turn your attention to your breath. Simply observe it flowing in and out of your body without trying to control it.

Now, as you breathe in, visualize yourself breathing in a brilliant white, healing light. And as you breathe out, send away any stresses, any negativity, anything bothering you.

Inhale that beautiful healing energy.

Exhale anything that does not serve you.

And as you continue to breathe in that wonderful healing energy, feel yourself becoming more and more relaxed.

Gradually, you become aware of the sound of rainfall. You realize that you are in the middle of a beautiful rain forest, surrounded by lush greenery. You hear the sounds of insects chirping, birds singing in the trees, while the rain pitter-patters down onto the leaves.

You walk through the trees, enjoying every sensation: the smell of the wet foliage and earth; the soothing sounds of the rain forest; the feel of the leaves brushing against you.

At last, you see a fallen tree up ahead, and you go and sit down next to it, resting your back against the tree. Closing your eyes, you lift your face up toward the sky, and you are overwhelmed by a beautiful feeling of gratitude. You are grateful for this moment. You are grateful for a place as peaceful as this. You are grateful for the blessings in your life. You are grateful for the blessings still to come. You are grateful for life itself.

And as you bask in this feeling of gratitude, you realize that this rain forest isn't just somewhere you can come to when you want to feel this strong sense of gratitude. It is part of you. It *is* you.

As you turn your attention back to your breath, watching it flow in and out, you know that you can come here any time you need.

This place is yours to enjoy whenever you need to remind yourself that peace and gratitude are your birthright, and you can access them whenever you need.

Start to wriggle your fingers, wriggle your toes. Stretch and yawn. And when you are ready, open your eyes.

8

I won't lie: the steps I cover in this chapter are not easy, and they do need some time to master. I still have a hard time controlling my emotions, and I'm far from perfect, but that should tell you that you don't have to do things perfectly for manifestation to work.

For example, I had a very annoying day today, and that's putting it mildly! A few weeks ago, I hired someone to do some work for me, and he stopped communicating with me. I'm a pretty easy-going guy, so I assumed there was a good reason for his behavior and gave him the benefit of the doubt.

However, after three weeks of tiptoe-ing around him with little change in his behavior, I was lost, upset, and frustrated with trying to get hold of him to no avail. He would show up for maybe an hour's work, then leave suddenly, leaving me hanging. Today, when I really needed his help, he did not pick up his phone or answer my messages.

My head was spinning with trying to figure out what to do for the best. I would have loved to be able to give him as long as he needed to pull himself together, but I had needs too. I couldn't do the work myself!

I hate sacking anyone I work with. I always feel bad about it, but I was running a business and sadly coming to the conclusion that I needed to hire someone else.

I was upset. I knew what needed to be done, but it still bothered me, knowing that I'd gone out of my way to support him, but all it had gotten me was delays, and the job still wasn't done.

My ego got a real kicking today, I can tell you. It was screaming at me, "That's not fair!"

I'm sharing this with you, so you can see that I have my bad days, just like you. I'm not going to give you the details of how I handled that guy, but I will tell you that things changed in a few short hours because I changed my mindset. As soon as the ego starts taking over my mind or stress seeps in, I shift my thoughts to gratitude and give thanks for what I have, not what I don't have.

I have clients who pay me and trust me.
I have the ability to support people who
are going through a hard time.
I have a plan B.
I know other suppliers and workmen
who can step in.
I have a stable home life.

As I switched my focus, things began to move the way I wanted, but it was hard work silencing those negative thoughts. I persisted, shifting my thoughts to gratitude and thanks, over and over again, talking to myself as I went about my day, going from job site to job site.

I also threw in some positive thinking by trying to find ways to solve the problem, taking responsibility for what I thought I could do in order to finish the project, instead of worrying about what was going on in that man's life or any other thoughts that wouldn't help solve the issue.

Again, this wasn't easy! My ego and all those negative emotions were lurking, just waiting to get out and mess with my mind, but I wasn't going to let them win.

On top of the positive thoughts, a few acts of kindness helped. In fact, it helped so much that an hour later, after I finished my last act of kindness for the day, I was able to solve the issue and have a good sleep.

Don't forget, tomorrow is always a new day, and today will become history. But in order for history to not repeat itself, you need to not make the same mistake you did last time. That simple. Remember, we mature not from time but from the hard times—the hurts, the mistakes, and the challenges.

But what I just shared with you is the easiest way to change your energy if you can't go to a quiet place and do a quick, powerful mantra meditation. Keep on repeating what you're grateful for, over and over again. This, combined with a few deep breaths, really, really helps.

And don't forget to throw in those acts of kindness. They don't need to be big. Doing good can be something as simple as opening a door for someone with a smile, letting someone in front of you in a line, leaving a tip when you get coffee, giving a few dollars to a homeless person, donating money to a dog shelter, or paying someone a compliment.

As soon as you do that, you will truly feel a shift in your day. And even better, by doing this over and over again, you will see a *shift in your life.*

Stop expecting to always get something in return. Do something because you want to do it, not because you need to or you *should*.

- You can choose to be happy.
- You can choose to enjoy life.
- You can choose to see the good in the bad.

I can go on and on and on.

If you want life to be fair, face the unfair, face your fear, and face those who block you or stop you from who you want to be or can be!

Mind Your Own Business

It's kind of funny to think about it now, but I used to love knowing about every little detail of other people's lives. Gossiping with friends was a part of my daily routine back then—posting a story, judging other people's stories, and getting jealous of other people—until one day I woke up and said, "I'm *out*!"

There were a few reasons I made this choice:

1. I realized I don't want people to know what I'm doing at any given moment; posting about my actions all the time was an act of attention seeking. I've noticed that unless you're using social media in this way, solely to grow your business, it will attract more negative than positive into your life.

2. Why do I care what other people, people who I barely know, are doing during the day?

3. If someone genuinely wants to know what I'm doing, they can call or text me, and those who don't have my number, well, I don't think they need to know my personal business.

4. I found that looking at other people's lives only pressured me to have a similar sort of life timeline, which might not be appropriate for me, and it just brought unnecessary anxiety to my life.

5. If you want to open a business, say, a bakery, in a street that already has one or two bakery stores, the only thing you need to do to succeed is believe in yourself and in your concepts. Keep the focus on *your* business, not theirs.

If you open a business out of fear, afraid you're not going to be able to compete, then what's the point of opening a business? Who cares how they run their business, how their pastries taste, and who they hire? Put all that energy into your business. Follow your own experience and instincts and find a way to perfect *your* thing. Businesses succeed in the most crowded of industries because the people behind them understand that there's plenty of abundance to go around. Thinking you have to fight your competitors for a slice of a tiny pie comes from a place of lack, and if you believe that you're going to struggle, you will.

Belief in yourself is the key to success. If you believe in yourself, you don't care about others who are not in your close circle. But even with close friends and family, you don't need to know every little detail of their business.

I'll say this again: if you come with the mindset that you *have* to make a change in your life, *stop right there!* You don't *have* to do shit! Saying you have to have or do something comes from a *negative mindset.*

When you instead say to yourself, "I want to make a change," you are starting from a *positive mindset.*

So, when things are not going as smoothly as you thought they would, if you have a positive mindset, you won't give up or see it as a failure, and you *will keep going* even if you have a setback. You keep going because you *want* to, not because you *have* to!

I have had my fair share of times when I was homeless because of bad choices, but during none of those times did I feel that in the end I wouldn't make it.

I won't lie. It was tough. When everyone in your circle is making more money and you've got nothing, it's not a good feeling! I've known all the feelings imaginable: loss of love, loss of friendship, loss of opportunity, loss of a home. But out of all of them, the worst loss was the loss of my way and my goals.

Just have faith, OK?

Get a small coin. Hold it between two fingers and straighten out your arm as far as you can. Look at your coin. It looks so small, right? So small it could be the moon far, far away.

Now keep focusing on the coin, and as you focus, start to bring the coin closer and closer to your eye. As the coin gets closer and closer to your eye, notice how the small coin shifts its size and gets bigger and bigger until it covers your eye, and you can't see anything!

What's the point behind this experiment? Well, the coin is a metaphor for our struggles and issues. We tend to put our focus on the *problems,* not giving our mind space to try to solve the issues, making a small problem bigger than it actually is. If only we could find a way to take a deep breath and focus on the big picture, like looking at the coin from far away, we would be able to make the adjustments we need.

Again, I am suggesting that you take responsibility for what you can, which is yourself; figure out what you're doing wrong, stop doing it, and move forward.

There is a saying: to get respect, you need to give respect. If you want respect from the Universe, you need to work on the inside of you, not the outside. I call it *king respect.* We are who we are, and we may as well accept that.

For some reason, we think if we get rich, all of our problems will disappear, and we'll finally be able to buy happiness. You think you'll be able to do a lot when you get rich, that everything will change. I used to get upset when people told me that money didn't mean a thing or matter in life, because the ones saying that had money! It's quite a different story and feeling when you *don't* have money.

It's so easy to say money doesn't matter when you don't need to worry about how you'll pay your rent!

In the end, though, I learned that they were right. Happiness comes from the inside. We all have a gift, which I call a candle waiting for us to light. Our struggles and wrong mindset keep us from lighting that candle, but we all have the power to experience that inner illumination. Light it up, guys!

Every decade, year, and minute, we are shaping ourselves into who we will become. Our choices and mistakes are the things that make us stronger and a better person, but they can just as easily make us sick and miserable by keeping us stuck in the past.

I didn't think that one day I would be writing a book or building a foundation to help others. My focus used to be, "I want to be successful so I can take care of my mom. I want to show everyone I can make it."

One of the reasons it took me so long to get to this point is because I was making the same mistakes as my mom, putting someone else's needs before mine. I was putting pressure on myself when things didn't go as smoothly as I had hoped, so I was unable to stay balanced and stable for a long time. I'd start something good, and then it would all fall apart again.

As soon as I began to stop and rethink my steps, I realized that I was fostering someone else's dreams, or, more accurately, sending the Universe the right idea but choosing the wrong path to get there.

Read and reread the following:

- Taking a step back from everyone is not a selfish act.
- Saying no or avoiding people to have space to work on yourself is not a selfish act!
- Not sharing your business with others until you reach the goals, you're happy with is not a selfish act.
- Thinking about your own needs before others when you're in the midst of seriously trying to build yourself is not a selfish act. It's called

healing! And don't forget: you can give so, so much more when you've healed yourself.

Exercise

Write a letter to yourself from two years in the future. Imagine you have achieved everything you've set out to achieve. What have you learned along the way? Who are you as a person now? What is your life like? What do you wish you'd learned sooner? What lessons would you like to teach your present self?

9

I once had to make a difficult choice. I had to choose between who I thought were friends for life or choose me. Actually, once I thought about it, it wasn't as hard as it seemed. For peace of mind, no ego, and no drama, guess what I chose?

I always defined friends as "people I know," and I know a *lot* of people. But as I started to consider the true nature of friendship, I realized that most of them weren't friends. For me, a friend should be someone who doesn't judge you or get jealous of you, who is loyal, trustworthy, and always there to support you, even if they disagree with your choices in life.

I see a friend as a part of my family, that no matter what, they're still family.

One time, I took a $1,000 loan from my brother to pay rent. Now, losing $1,000 wasn't going to change his life if I didn't give it back, but when I asked for the loan, I told my brother that my boss promised me he'd pay me the next week, and I'd pay his money back then.

Unfortunately, my boss didn't pay me when he said he would, so I wasn't able to keep my word, and my brother wouldn't speak to me as a consequence.

Eventually, I was able to pay him back. It took some time, but I did pay him back. I remember telling my mom how stupid he was to stop talking to me over the loan. "I mean, I'm his brother! Like no matter how he looks at it, we're blood."

That's how I view a friend, so these days, I don't have many people I can call friends.

I learned a lot from that loan from my brother. Overcoming pain and failures can become a positive power and can help us move forward from our limitations. If you stay in pain, not facing your issues or learning from them, you will continue to live in pain, empowering negativity and attracting it over and over into your life. No! You've got to stop the cycle.

I'll give you an example. I love my mom and know she wants the best for me. The thing is, every time I tell her something positive that's happening, or an opportunity I have, she finds a way to be negative about it.

Do you know someone like that in your life? It's pretty common and can be a real downer when you're trying to move forward. However, one of the reasons she does this is because she isn't happy with her own life right now and is sadly stuck in her past failures, and instead of letting it go, she tends to bring down others.

Another reason people do this is to protect you from disappointment, especially if they have suffered disappointments in their own lives. They see your high hopes and fear for you if you don't succeed.

However, because of her own bias, my mother's advice isn't relevant to me, so now I prefer telling her good news when it's official. If I'm honest, I used to be one of those people, so now when someone comes to me with an idea or wants to change, I am conscious of not wanting to undermine their hard work. Instead, I ask them, "Are you happy? Will it change your life in a better way?"

Did you ever grow up saying, "I will never be like my mom or dad!"? I did! And oh, we promise ourselves that we will never make the same mistakes, never use the same methods they used when trying to teach us what was good and bad.

If we stop and think for a moment, if we *are* like them (and it's a rare individual who is nothing like their parents), we can either accept it, or we can change and adjust ourselves to be more like how we want to be.

So, stop for a second and ask yourself three questions:

- How did I get to this point?
- How can I change this?
- How do I face my past?

As soon as you acknowledge your heritage and see the similarity between you and your parents, you will be able to change and start a new chapter in your life. Acceptance goes a long way.

As spiritual beings, we are in the material world to fulfil a particular purpose. Many of us have no idea what our greater purpose is, so we give up on life or choose the wrong way, all because of those walls and struggles we are facing in life. We simply must *know* that life is providing us with clues about our larger purpose, which often come in the form of struggle and life's difficult or "bad" situations.

Since I moved to NYC, all my dad has been able to say to me is the only sentence he knows in English: "Don't give up." I guess he knows that there have been lots of moments in my life when I wanted to give up, asking what the point of life was when it was nothing but struggle after struggle, any glimpses of happiness snatched away at the last minute. What's the point of falling in love and then feeling the pain of a broken heart?

But from all those situations, I learned one big thing: the reason the pain was stronger than I was. *It was because I didn't believe in myself.* I didn't believe that something better was coming or that small changes were all that were needed for things to work out.

There are a lot of couples who get divorced and a few years later get married again. Why? Because at that time, both sides needed to work on themselves for some time and being together was stopping them from doing so.

It's important to keep your eyes open to *all* possibilities because life will use all sorts of ways to help you fulfil your purpose. However, much as it pains me to say it, you probably won't find it with flowers and hugs. Like most successful people, you are more likely to find it with struggles and pain. But why? Why does it have to be that way? Well, because not all of us can see what is in front of us and determine if it's a good or bad choice. Sometimes we make good choices but execute them badly. It's like the Universe gives us a slap in the face so we don't do it again.

At the end of the day, if you have a goal in your life, or goals, if you work for them, you *will* get there, no matter what. The question isn't if but when. How fast will it take you to get there? If I didn't change my mindset, then getting to my goals would have taken much longer. If you start your transformation today and are persistent, slowly, slowly you will begin to see a change. And one day, that slow movement will become faster and faster.

One of the big reasons why the change occurs is because you remove the blocks of stress and fear as you feel more confident on your new path. What was once stressful becomes better than the day before, the week before, the month before when it was *really* hard. You start to notice the people you meet on the street are smiling at you. People want to talk to you. The coffee spot around the corner serves you a free coffee, not just once but every day. Girls start talking to you while you're busy reading a book. You start to feel good about yourself, and as you do, the loneliness disappears, with you being friendlier to the world around you.

You feel like a celebrity. *You feel a change!* And now you can't avoid it; you've got to keep going because you've built momentum.

As you start to see things different-ly, you'll want to feed yourself with new knowledge, spiritually and in business. With stress and fear out of the way, your mind and body are energized to go and get what you want. You may start to want to do more for yourself and for others but without expecting anything in return. This is the level. This is it, guys! And why are you happy to give without expectations? Because you know that the Universe has got your back if you do!

I feel like now's a good time to remind you that I promised you something at the end of this book, something that will hopefully give you the drive to dive even deeper into the idea of the law of attraction.

Even if you've tried and it didn't work before, I promise you, this time, you'll feel a change. Just try it one last time, OK?

Exercise

I want you to do a visualization exercise with me.

Close your eyes and imagine you have all the money you've ever wanted and more. Your roof has developed a leak. How much of a problem is this for you?

Not much, right? You're a millionaire! All you have to do is pay someone to fix it, and you've got the money to do that.

Now imagine you don't have any money at all. You're struggling to pay a bill and don't know how you're going to manage until the end of the month. Your roof develops a leak. How much of a problem is it now?

It's a *major* problem!

This exercise shows you that it's all about perspective. Problems are only as big or as small as you perceive them to be, and believe it or not, most problems are smaller than you think. As you enter into a flow state with the Universe, you discover more and more creative ways of dealing with any issue. For example, maybe you meet someone who fixes roofs, and they need help with their website. Websites are your jam! You agree to make them a brand-new website in exchange for fixing your roof.

You didn't need money after all. You just needed to be open to possibility and understand that problems are only as big as you make them.

10

I have a funny story about the time I was sharing an apartment with my brother, who is very into yoga and his morning runs. That last year we lived together in that apartment was one of the worst times of my life.

I'd stopped going to the gym. Instead, I wanted to focus on my work because I had responsibilities, and I could feel my life going downhill. I knew I was about to lose my company to my partners. I knew I was about to lose my girlfriend, and there was nothing I could do about it except search for an answer to fix it all.

It was hard, because I was fighting with my mind to not point fingers at anyone besides myself and my choices, but I was still having plenty of fear-based thoughts, so all I was seeing was block after block.

The one thing I was able to hold onto was my diet. I'd started intermittent fasting, and maybe because it was the one thing under my control, I managed to observe it, breaking my fasting before time. Meanwhile, my brother was maintaining his work and workout schedule.

All I did was go to work, then come home and either watch TV or stay in my room. Maybe I'd do the occasional abs class at the gym, but I certainly wasn't diligent about exercising. Despite this, I was becoming fitter and fitter while losing weight, while my brother was gaining it! Even his girlfriend commented on how my brother was getting bigger, which really upset him.

One night, I made dinner for my brother and his girlfriend, and as we were eating, my brother asked me what my secret was. I sent him Thomas's videos and explained a few things he needed to do to start fasting, and that was it. He was hooked.

Now my brother is forty-nine years old but looks ten years younger.

So, I recommend you look into this diet and give it a try. You'll even find it will help clear your mind and allow you to think more clearly. The best part is that this diet won't stop you from eating what you love as long as you break your fast the right way and eat according to Thomas's instructions.

I remember very clearly when I first discovered intermittent fasting. I was going through YouTube one day when an ad came up for an intermittent fasting program. Thomas Delaure was explaining this type of diet and the benefits of it. He broke it down so beautifully that I just had to give it a try. If you're struggling with weight, I really recommend following him.

His story goes something like this: "I was fat, eating more than I should, trying all of the diets in the world, but nothing worked. I had no confidence, I was about to quit, but then I tried this diet, and look at me now!"

With intermittent fasting, you don't really have to go to the gym, but if you do combine it with exercise, you'll see faster results. The basic premise is you fast for sixteen hours of the day and have a window of eight hours to eat. However, the most important part of this fasting is *how* you break your fast. If you follow Thomas's videos, he will break it down for you, including various options for different diets, such as vegetarian.

During fasting, there are a few things you're allowed to do to help you respect your fast, such as consuming the following:

- black coffee or green or black tea with no sugar
- water
- hot lemon water (which I drink in the morning before anything else)
- apple cider vinegar mixed with water or one shot a day
- pink salt mixed in water, tea, or black coffee

Now, I want to break down just how good this diet is for your body. The sixteen hours of fasting gives your body the time it needs to support each part of your body and break down food the right way. Once you start fasting, you'll find you have more power and energy once you get past the first month or so. (Although each body differs, so it may take you more or less time.) I can assure you that when I share this diet with anyone, once they experience the benefits, they never give it up and are still doing it, like me.

The word *breakfast* comes from *break* and *fast* because you sleep at night for however many hours, and then when you wake up, you eat, breaking your nighttime fast.

The time when you break your fast isn't as important as *how* you break it. Your body is very sensitive at this time, so pay attention to the first thing you put in your mouth.

Here's my tip: do not break your fast with a big meal! Try to eat something light like rice cakes, seaweed snacks, and blubbery. For those who eat meat, you can add a small, plain piece of grilled chicken breast, salmon, or beef without oil, salt, or flavorings. You should never break a fast with carbs because that will spike your insulin, putting your body into shock mode, increasing your insulin fat.

If you eat a heavy meal after fasting for six to eight hours of sleep, your body will triple the usual amount of insulin it produces, creating more fat instead of breaking it down. So, you want to eat something small and simple, just to satisfy the craving for food.

Since diet isn't the main remit of this book, if you want to learn more about this approach to diet, follow Thomas or any other fitness expert you feel comfortable with. (And remember to consult a medical professional before making any major changes to your diet and exercise regime.) Thomas breaks it down in scientific ways that make it much easier to understand.

Exercise

Go to YouTube and watch some of Thomas's videos. Start putting what you learn into practice and journal the results. You'll soon see the difference, which will help you understand that you can make little changes to your life but get a big result, a principle you can apply to everything you do.

11

Over the years, the Universe sent me many signs about the fact that I was going to live in New York. It started when I was twelve years old, rooting for the New York Knicks when everyone else was cheering for the Chicago Bulls. My mom wanted to send me to NYC to live with her cousin if I could be accepted at the high school my brothers and sister went to, a plan that sadly failed to come to fruition. My good friend at the time was always bragging about NYC and her trips to NYC.

I started to really feel those signs affecting my thoughts about NYC when I was working in London, trying to make extra money, and considering staying in London. I was working on the street selling Nokia cell phone covers and holiday socks in an outdoor shopping mall, freezing my ass off day after day just to make a few bucks.

One day, two women with five kids approached my cart, asking me to give each one of them something for free. I tried to explain that what I was selling didn't belong to me, so anything I gave away would come out of my pocket. My words didn't seem to register, and they were so persistent, so eventually I found myself giving them all some free things, wishing them happy holidays.

Suddenly, one of the women asked for my hand, saying, "Let me see your future."

Thoughts were swirling in my mind: *Leave me alone! You got what you wanted, so off you go!* But something made me give her my hand.

She looked at my palm and, I kid you not, said, "You do not belong here. You should go to NYC; you will be successful there."

The *really* big sign appeared when I was working in an airport, and I met my NYC-bragging friend before she got on a flight to London. She convinced me to go with her to NYC after she returned. Since I was getting those flights for free, I figured, *Why not?*

I called my cousin and told her I was coming with my friend. I set up a date, and we arrived between Christmas and the new year, the perfect time for shopping.

As soon as I got to NYC, I had this feeling, a *massive* energy. I can't quite explain it, but the sensation was so powerful that at the end of the trip, I told my cousin to wait for me, because I was coming back. Sure enough, I went back to my spiritual home, and the rest, as they say, is history.

I'm sharing these moments because either we don't see the signs, or, if we do, we ignore them. Looking back at the time when my mom was planning to send me to NYC, I might regret that she didn't. But instead, I'm grateful that the Universe persisted in showing me the direction and for my ability to pick up on these signs, understand them, and believe in them.

Sometimes, the thing that appears so obvious with hindsight we dismiss as nonsense. If we could listen to those signs, think how different life could be.

One of the reasons we avoid these signs is because we're distracted by our issues or other people's problems. We give up so many opportunities because we're too busy thinking about how it will affect other people instead of seeing how it would lift us up.

These days, I often ask myself, "Who am I to help others when I can't even help myself? What good will it do to see someone else happy when I am miserable?" We pretend that our thoughts and feelings don't matter, and we can be happy for someone else even while we're stuck in pain or failure.

It's not true! Of *course,* your feelings matter, and it's impossible to be truly happy for someone else when you're unhappy yourself. It's like going to work when you're sick; you still give 100 percent, but your 100 percent when you're ill is the equivalent of 20–30 percent of the power you have when you're fine. That's how you can measure how happy you can feel for someone else when you're not happy.

How is all this related to seeing signs? Easy. Now that I'm closer to where I want to be, I can look back over all the signs in my life, all the ups and downs, and understood how I got to where I am today. Knowing what I missed back then makes it easier for me to notice when the Universe is sending me a sign now. I can see signs on any given day, both bad and good days.

If you can start to find happiness and gratitude for things that you already have and the things you are manifesting, you will see your signs. Even better, if you can see the signs, you'll be able to act on them to harness their power to elevate your life.

I suggest looking out for Gabby Bernstein's books *Spiritual Attraction* or *The Universe Has Your Back*. She suggests some excellent ways of how you can work with your signs.

The reason I'm writing this book is to share my point of view on the law of attraction. No one can fully explain why it works, but somehow the Universe knows what needs to be changed in our lives to see results, and countless people have used that power to manifest everything they want. There *is* a reason why there are a million books written about this topic! But regardless of the author, we all bring our own interpretation to the table in the hope we can help someone. All I can do is be myself, and if what I'm saying and the way I'm saying it resonates with you, then I've achieved my goal!

Look at my brother, for example. He was working out *so* hard, running five to ten miles every day and doing daily yoga classes before COVID-19 hit.

Seeing me not doing a thing *and* losing weight was driving him crazy! There he was, doing all that hard work, sweating it out, yet seeing worse results than I was! It doesn't make sense, right?

Well, it does once you know the secret. You see, my brother believed that when it comes to being successful, *you must work hard.* He's not wrong, but from his perspective, I wasn't working hard to lose weight. What he couldn't see was that I *was* working hard. Maintaining a diet is no easy task. Most of us fail sooner or later. It looks easy on paper, but in real life, intermittent fasting in its early stages is not that easy, especially when you're depressed and you feel like things aren't going your way. It takes a lot of discipline and will power to maintain any diet you choose to do under these circumstances. But when you *know* it's going to be worth the work and sacrifice, when you believe with every aspect of your being that it's going to pay off, it's easier to stay on the path.

My goal is to make you believe in yourself. I've mentioned this before, and I'll continue to do so. I like bugging you! We're all special in our own way; we just need to find it in ourselves, find our purpose. I don't want you to wait for someone else to direct you; all you may need is for me to give you a push in the right direction, and then you can do the rest.

The fact that you are reading this book means that you are a believer in the spiritual side of life. In fact, reading this is your *third* sign that you are on the right path! The first was the cover that attracted your attention, and the second were the words on the back of the book that spoke to you. These are all signs that you are asking for help from some sort of power. I want to show you a few tricks that can help you become a better interpreter of these signs.

I was just like you, all alone and ready to give up, tired of trying and trying and trying. Then COVID-19 happened, and I noticed something weird. Unlike the people around me, I wasn't worried.

Besides the mask we now had to wear, I was pretty much doing everything else in my daily routine like normal. I'm kind of OCD already when it comes to cleaning. People have compared me to Monica from the show *Friends*, but now instead of mocking me, they started to understand why it was so important to keep everything spotless.

In addition, I felt as if COVID-19 gave me the opportunity to work on myself in the way that I needed to instead of putting it off, just like my mom avoiding going to the doctor to check her breasts to see if she had cancer. It took an accident to put her in the hospital and get her body examined to figure that out. Thanks to an unknown power, my mom got a second chance in life. The pandemic was my wake-up call, and it can be yours too, if you let it.

COVID-19 was a low point for a lot of us, but we can't undo what happened. What we can do is learn and adjust ourselves— that is, if you feel that you should. Only you know what needs to change.

But please, let go of the past! You can't change it, guys. You can only change the *now*. You can't know what is going to happen tomorrow. All you can do is this:

- Control your actions.
- Focus on yourself before helping your friends or family.

- Find out what makes you happy— the kind of happiness that lasts, not for an hour or a few hours, so you can keep doing it day after day after day.
- Balance your heart with your mind, and don't let one control the other.
- Find the alignment within your well-being.
- Stop looking for others to approve of your actions.
- Don't be afraid to fail.

Michael Jordan didn't become a six-time champion as soon as he joined the NBA. It took him seven to eight years before he got his first ring. That means that for eight years in the league, he failed to reach his goal. He isn't any different from you or me, even though he's an international sports star. What sets him apart is that he kept going, built the muscles in his body, corrected his game, made a coaching change, and did whatever it took to reach his goal. He added a key player who helped him win. He made adjustments in his life and in his game. He didn't just wing it. And I don't think it was any coincidence that MJ was around someone who was knowledgeable in Zen philosophy.

One of the main principles of Zen philosophy is that you do things in small steps in order to make a big change. For example, if you want to use a treadmill, don't set out with the intention of being on it for forty-five minutes. You'll find it hard to keep going, so you'll give up and then feel like a failure because you didn't stick with it. Instead, start by telling yourself you'll do three minutes, then do another five minutes and another. Watch a favorite show or listen to something to keep your mind off of looking at the timer. Slowly, slowly, and without realizing it, you'll have been on the treadmill for forty-five minutes!

This Zen idea is so much more than what I can go into here, so if you want to know more, I really recommend you check out *One Small Change Can Change Your Life* by Robert Maurer. Zen is all about asking the small questions instead of the big one you can't answer. Taking small actions and thinking small thoughts solves small problems, showing you how to change what looks like a big, insurmountable problem, making it a small, more manageable one. This way, you can change behaviors that are blocking your brain from seeing the things that *can* be solved.

All of the tips and advice in books are great, but in the end, it's the doing that creates the change. You can read ten thousand books, but if you aren't putting what you learn into practice, it just won't work.

Let's look at life for a minute as if it were a sports game. You have the players and the coaching staff. Before the game in the locker room, the coaches will do a tactic briefing, go over the positions of each player opening the game, and then the coach and his staff will build up the players' confidence to get into the game.

They will tell you various things:

- Don't let the situations in the game affect your game.
- Always keep playing.
- Build momentum by pressing the ball or players.
- Ignore other players' trash talk.

If you look at those tips, you'll see I'm trying to tell you the same things; or really, it's the Universe trying to tell you:

- Don't let the situation in the game affect your game; don't let issues or the obstacles along the way stop you from reaching your goals.
- Keep playing; keep moving along. Keep striving. Don't stop.
- Build momentum by pressing the ball or player; work on yourself and press toward your dreams.
- Don't listen to other players' trash talk and let it get to your head. Don't let others tell you what you can and can't do or convince you not to follow your dreams.

At halftime, if the team is losing, the coach will then work on the mental side of the players. They'll analyze the team's mistakes and suggest how to make a change. I could go on and on, but mostly I want to say this:

- The game of life is not over. We still have time to play!
- We start the second half 0–0. We can always start fresh.

This last sentence is the key for the next half, for the rest of your lives. You can't change what's already happened, but you *can* change the now. The second half is what's still to come, which offers an opportunity to make a change. Who doesn't love a fresh start? You can give yourself one today!

If you need to let go of other players/friends, then so be it. The end game is to win, so do what is best for the club/team, and the club/team is *you*.

Nothing comes easily at the beginning of a change, especially if you have kids/family. Finding the balance between your obligations to them and what you want to do for yourself will be hard. But *it is possible* for those who truly want it. You'll make it work, you'll prioritize, and you'll find the time. It really is all about how much you want your dream life.

How much do you want to feel good almost every day? How much do you want to be able to see opportunities that pass others by?

As soon as you can answer those questions by yourself, and feel committed to this new course, you will be able to start your first half of the game from 0–0.

Don't forget: throughout the second half of the game (the rest of your life), you've got to keep working. So, when you manifest your dream life, don't let your ego or your fears take over. Keep doing what you've done to get to that point.

Some food for thought from some of the most successful, influential men around:

*Everything you want is on
the other side of fear.*

—Jack Canfield

*Everything negative, pressure
and challenges, are all an
opportunity for me to rise.*

—Kobe Bryant

*I learned that courage was not the
absence of fear, but the triumph over it.
The brave man is not he who does not
feel afraid but he who conquers that fear.*

—Nelson Mandela

Fear is a powerful force that somehow does not allow many people to get what they want in life.

—David Schwartz

I could go on and on, showing you how successful people have struggled and sacrificed and faced fear. I like to remind myself that I'm not alone in feeling this way, so once a week, and also when I'm feeling down, I look for quotes from famous people to lift my vibration. Everyone who had a dream faced the same issues in their lives, or battles in their minds, just like me and just like you.

At the end of the day, you are only really dealing with yourself, the voice in your head, the overthinking; the physical world is just a game. Maybe you've seen *The Truman Show* with Jim Carrey, where he is living his life for the entertainment of others without even realizing it. At the end of the movie, he breaks out of the set, escaping the limitations of his environment, to face his fear of what's out there and discovers there is much more to life than he could have imagined.

Jim Carrey in the movie changed his daily routine, and slowly, slowly, saw clues that opened his eyes to the truth—that there was more to this bubble he was in. There was more in him and more *for* him if he changed his reality by facing his fears and stepping out of his comfort zone. At the beginning of the movie, everything seemed normal to him, until he was able to notice the signs that were always there but that he couldn't see because he was too comfortable in the reality he was stuck in.

That's how most of us are, living the same old lives day to day, until we feel this push in ourselves, that inner part of us saying, "I deserve better, and I can be better."

Observing that push is the first step, but for many, it stops there. Why? Why are we afraid to make that move or change? Even that *small* move, that *small* change?

Maybe it's because it feels so overwhelming, but no one told you that you have to do it all in one shot. Start your change slowly. Take small steps. Build your confidence in yourself gradually, till you feel comfortable in betting on yourself. You'll get there.

There is a funny story about a guy who was having trouble in his love life. He decided to see a psychiatrist to try to figure out what was wrong with him.

The psychiatrist asked the guy, "What's the issue?"

"Well," said the guy, "I'm having trouble finding a girl to marry."

"Why is that?" asked the psychiatrist.

"Because every girl I bring home, my mom dislikes. She keeps saying I need a woman like her! I'm not sure what to do."

The psychiatric asked the guy, "Do you love how your mom looks?"

"Yes."

"Do you like your mom's personality?"

"Yes, I love her personality!"

"Do you love every bit of your mom?"

"Are you kidding me? Of course! That's why it's so hard to find someone like my mom."

"I tell you what," said the psychiatrist. "Go to your mom and tell her that if she wants you to marry a girl like herself, she should find you one."

The guy liked this idea, so when he returned home, he told his mom what the psychiatrist told him to do. Seven months later, the guy was back at the psychiatrist's, who asked him, "Did your mom manage to find someone like herself?"

"She did! It was amazing! It was like seeing a younger version of my mom. It was unbelievable how similar they were—how they talked, walked, dressed, thought just the same!"

"So, did you get married?"

"Oh no!" replied the guy.

"Why not?"

"Well, now my *dad* doesn't like her!"

The point of this story is for you to stop living someone else's life or dream! Think of all those people who became doctors or lawyers because it was what their parents wanted, and now they're miserable. I was caught in this illusion for nine years, always doing something to please someone else, kidding myself that I was happy.

If you are playing the game to please someone else, stop! This is *your* life, your only life. Only adapt and change if *you* want to. The only thing you should fear is making choices that make you miserable. Your kids are not going to look down on you if you follow your dreams; they will admire you and learn from you how to create their dream life. Your family doesn't own or understand what is going on in your head, not even your husband or wife. All they can do is support your efforts to better yourself, and if they can't, well then, they can move on along and out of your life!

So, what's the trick? How can you face your negative thoughts in order to manifest more positive ones? How can you change this negative energy on a bad day?

I mentioned a few things before that help me immensely, but I'm going to summarize them here for you to make sure you fully appreciate them:

- Don't fight bad thoughts or energy. Observe those thoughts. Understand that we are all human and being upset is normal. Some of those feelings can be the result of your environment. For example, something frustrating has occurred, or someone has upset you. These moments do not have to change your life. Feel how you feel, but don't get stuck. Shift the thoughts before they take over your day.

- Move your thoughts swiftly to ones of gratitude. Be thankful for this moment, thankful for your dreams and goals, thankful for what you have and what you will manifest in your life.

- Grab your headphones and press play on your happy playlist. Get pumped by your favorite song that always puts a smile on that beautiful face of yours. Yes, you are beautiful!

Exercise

Make a list of negative experiences in your life. What happened? What happened as a consequence? How did your life improve? What lessons did you learn? How can you use those experiences to build a better life?

Now close your eyes and spend a few moments in meditation. As you inhale, think about one of the items on your list. As you exhale, give thanks to the Universe for the opportunity it gave you to know and do better.

When you have finished working through your list, spend a minute or two sitting in pure gratitude for everything that has happened to bring you to this moment. When you are done, thank the Universe for all the blessings it has sent to you and all the blessings still to come.

12

When you shift your life toward happiness, joy, and gratitude, you will see a shift in many areas. This shift can catch you by surprise with how quickly it can hit. In less than a month, you should already be able to see the changes.

My grandpa passed away when I was around ten years old. I remember asking my mom, "Who is going to stay and take care of Grandma now that Grandpa is not around?"

My mom answered, "No one."

So, I told my mom, "Then I will."

My mom didn't really mind the idea. My grandma's house wasn't far from ours, and she could see that it would make my life a bit easier not being around the issues my mom and dad were facing at the time. At first, I couldn't really do much to help my grandma, since I was only ten. That changed as I got older, and over the years, my grandma and I shared a strong bond. I'll admit that I wasn't an easy kid growing up, but Grandma didn't seem to care. I have a big family, and I'm sure I was her favorite! When I was away in the army or in London, my mom's sister tried to take over my room, but my grandma wouldn't let her. It was the same when I moved to NYC. She was always hoping I would come back, so she kept my room as an option for me.

When I left to go to NYC, my whole family started to fall apart. When my grandma died, and those Friday nights at Grandma's, where we all got together to connect, died with her. My grandma was that vital piece of the puzzle who kept us all together.

When I decided to move to NYC, people thought it just another one of those crazy ideas of mine, that I would be back in less than a month. My dad, when he got his life together, bought me a car—a brand-new car that to this day is still sitting in his parking lot, barely used. I drove the car for two years, maybe three, and left for NYC.

How do all these tales from my life have a connection to miracles? Good question. I'm glad you asked. What I'm about to share with you is one of the many miracles we all experience but pay little attention to.

At the time, I was in NYC working for a renovation company, driving my van in Brooklyn to pick up some materials.

There was heavy rain, the kind of rain that leaves the window wipers useless. On top of it, I was sick with a fever. My eyes were burning, and my throat was awfully sore, but I didn't take a day off because I'm not that kind of person. My parents taught me you should always go to work, no matter what.

While I was driving, I got a call on my cell from Grandma's number. One of my cousins was on the line and told me Grandma had passed away. I broke down as soon as she told me. I'd promised my grandma I would see her before she passed away, and I hadn't been able to. I'm the kind of guy who always keeps my word, even if it takes a while, but I failed to keep my word to one of the most amazing people in the world, the love of my life!

As soon as I heard the news, I hung up on my cousin and sobbed. It was as if my heart just couldn't take it, as if it wanted to disconnect from my body.

I don't remember how long I was crying for. What I do remember, though, is that as soon as I stopped, I wasn't sick. None of the symptoms I mentioned above were there anymore. Not one! I felt powerful. I felt healthy. I felt like my grandma had taken the pain from me, giving me a sign to keep going and letting me know she was there watching over me.

So, yes, I believe in miracles. I believe we should expect and accept miracles. I mean, what is the point of turning to the Universe and asking for help if you don't expect to get that help in return? What is the point of asking for forgiveness or asking for a sign? We all believe there is something out there bigger than ourselves. Something magical, some higher power. Even those who say they don't believe in

God, Jesus, or Mohammad still believe in something; they just give it a different name.

Think about this: the soul has come to the body, and the body to life, for the purpose of evolution. You are evolving and becoming. And you are using your relationship with everything around you to decide what you are becoming.

This is what you were born to do. This is the *joy* of creating your *self*. Of knowing your *self*. Of becoming, consciously, what you wish to be, what the world needs you for. It is what is meant by being *self*-conscious. You are here in the relative world so that you might have the tools with which to know and experience *who you really are*. And *who you are* is who you create yourself to be in relationship to the rest of the world. Often, we do not remember *who we are* and do not know *who we want to be* until we try out a few new ways of being. That is why honoring your truest feelings is so important.

Are there things in your life you'd like to change? We never know how much time we have left. But your life can still be changed immensely no matter how many days you have left on this earth. You just need to do the following:

- Slow down enough to consider what is true and real.
- Always try to understand the way other people feel.
- Be slow to anger.
- Show more appreciation.
- Love the people in your life as you've never loved them before.
- Treat others with respect.
- And wear a smile more often.

We need to do all of the above so that when our eulogy is read, when our life's actions are shared, we can be proud of the things said and how we spent our lives.

What will your choices be today? From this day forward, let us remember that many will not know when their last moment is. One moment, many loved ones are with us, and the next moment, they are gone.

Exercise

Make a list of the times when someone was there for you. It could be something as simple as someone holding the door open for you while you were carrying something heavy, or it could be when a friend or relative was there for you during a tough time. Maybe it was a teacher at school who taught you how to read or write or an employer who trained you in the skills you needed to do your job.

How many times have people helped you? It can be difficult to acknowledge this at times, but when we start being conscious of how we have been supported by the Universe our whole life, we can become more aware of the miracles that happen every single day.

Meditate and visualize the faces of everyone who has supported you. Give thanks to the Universe for their presence in your life and for all the people still to come who will be another miracle in your life.

*Fuck your past, date your present
and keep flirting with your future.*

—Vishal Painkra

13

Many of us take regular showers and try to look our best. We style our hair and care about our appearance. If we're not happy with something, we change the color of our hair, get a haircut, maybe get Botox to smooth out the lines on our face, or go for a wax. All of those physical changes are, for some reason, easy for us to make. Book it in, get it done. Feel better until the novelty wears off and we're unhappy with ourselves again.

We often have something about our appearance we want to change or are unhappy with. As a kid, I was bothered by the amount of hair I had, thinking I had to shave everything off to get girls to like me. Believing this was the reason I wasn't getting the girls is just one of the stupid things I had going on in my head.

Looking back at those pictures of myself as young kid, I just feel shocked to think of how stupid I was. I was actually a good-looking kid, and I was told this, but I didn't believe it because I wasn't able to get the girls. With hindsight, I realize that I didn't get the girls in school, but in high school, they were all over me!

The point I'm trying to make is to think about everything you go through to change your physical appearance. When you do it for the first time, it's painful. But as you get used to the pain, you learn to embrace it, knowing how much you love the end result.

Why can you put up with pain and discomfort to improve your physical appearance and not do the same for your inner being? The rewards are bigger too; any real, lasting external change comes from this inner work. Indeed, you may even cut back on those physical changes once you start on your spiritual journey because you will realize how you don't need them anymore.

Why? Because you start loving yourself! You'll stop caring so much about what others think of you, knowing that those around you love you for who you are. They love your heart and soul, and what could be better? And the others? The ones who don't love you? *Who gives a fuck what they think?*

One thing you can do to your appearance that will definitely make you more attractive and happier is wear a smile!

Have you ever had someone tell you to cheer up and smile? It's probably not the most welcome advice, and most of us tend to get even more upset when someone says it, especially when we're feeling sick, tired, or just plain down in the dumps.

But what if I told you that there's actually a good reason to turn that frown upside down? Science has shown that the mere act of smiling can lift your mood, lower stress, boost your immune system, and possibly even prolong your life. In other words, smiling can trick your brain into believing you are happy, which can then spur real feelings of happiness. Pretty cool.

But it doesn't end there. An ENT-otolaryngologist in Los Angeles points to the science of psychoneuroimmunology (the study of how the brain is connected to the immune system), asserting that it has been shown over and over again that depression weakens our immune system, while happiness, on the other hand, has been shown to boost our body's resistance. The simple physical act of smiling can make a difference in building your immunity because when you smile, the brain feels the muscles and assumes that something good is happening. So even forcing a fake smile can legitimately reduce stress and lower your heart rate! When you smile, your brain releases tiny molecules called neuropeptides to help fight off stress. Then other neurotransmitters like dopamine, serotonin, and endorphins come into play too.

There are plenty of smiling people who can testify to the fact that it helps them get through the day. A smile is also something that's easy to pass on. Much like yawning, smiling is contagious, which I love.

The reason smiling is contagious is because of the intention and feeling behind that smile. When someone smiles at you, you feel the good vibes from them, which makes you want to pass a smile on to the next person, and so on.

If we cannot face ourselves, our mindset, and our fears, we are going to limit our potential for any kind of real growth. Self-change is not easy, and it hurts, just like waxing does! But if it's worth it to you, you'll keep going when the going gets tough. Self-change is like having a laser treatment. It hurts a bit, but in the end, the result is worth it. Why not spend your time or money on real happiness, instead of paying for clothes or physical changes that only last a week, month, or a year before you have to do it all again?

So, What Makes You *Really* Happy?

By now, you should know what you want from life, and hopefully, bit by bit, you are getting rid of the bad habits preventing you from moving forward.

Think about whether those habits *really* make you happy, or is it that you think they *should* make you happy? Or perhaps they did make you happy a decade ago, but you have evolved.

When I got to this stage, I realized just how much I love staying home or in my area, which is very different from the party lifestyle I used to enjoy. People change! I never imagined I'd love to wake up in the morning, meditate, drink my hot water with lemon, and then pray. Yet here I am, loving life more than ever before. I hit the gym, then stop by the coffee spot near my building, where I get my warm, happy *good morning* from the staff who are now my friends. I get my coffee for free, since I'm so generous with my tips, along with my unique energy and smile, and I settle down to read a few pages of my super-interesting life-improving books while I enjoy my drink. What a life! By the time I'm ready to check my emails, I've started my workday from a happy place.

What else did I realize makes me happy? What else did I decide was essential in my daily life? Well, riding my bike makes me feel like a kid again. I love riding from the Upper West all the way down to Soho on the Hudson side, stopping in at the Dominic Bakery, where I get my free coffee and sweets. Yes, free! When you give, you receive. It's just how it works.

I make sure I enjoy time with my family and close friends, but I no longer go out like I used to. These days, every day is a weekend feeling for me. But I'll get to that in a minute.

There's another thing that happens when you get to this point. I started helping the homeless. As I mentioned earlier, this book is going to do good, by helping you and your friends and by giving back to the community. There are many, many homeless people who simply made bad choices, or had some bad luck, and didn't get a second chance. I'm going to be their second chance. With your help, I want to share this book. I want to share how much good it can bring. I want everyone to feel as good as I do now, and I know they can do it because I did it.

I also want to be able to help kids whose parents can't afford education or medical support. I'm donating a percentage of the profit of this book, starting with

18 percent (18 means "Hai" or life). As the book sells more and more, then the percentage of what I can use to help others will grow too, until I can give 90 percent, which is five times the number eighteen. Five times mean "Hamsa," which protects against the evil eye. I've got it sorted!

I've just shared with you what makes me happy, but let's look at what makes *you* happy. When I was trying to figure out the things that make me happy, I tried everything I could think of until I got a strong feeling of fulfilment. I used to hate reading, or I *thought* I hated reading. Now, it's one of my favorite things to do.

So, have an open mind. Simply because you didn't like or weren't good at something before doesn't mean you can't give it another go. Listen to your gut. Surprise yourself. I was so surprised when a book was able to draw me right in and the rush of knowledge was so strong. I had no idea I could enjoy it so much. Before, I was reading maybe one book a year and only in the summer. Now, there are too many books and too little time!

I realized the reason I wasn't drawn to reading wasn't because of a lack of time but because of past issues and fears. As soon as I had overcome some problems by facing them, I realized how curious I was. I wanted to know more, and more, and more! I love how reading opens my mind, even if 80 percent of the book is stuff I already know. That 20 percent of valuable information I didn't know can make a big impact.

I highly recommend you find those books that can help you be a better you, or that can help you see the big picture in life. Books that inspire and challenge you, books that soothe and comfort you. Books that make you smile and feel less alone in your struggles.

I truly hope that my book will do the same, and that is the key reason I wrote it. I want to help you by sharing my story, because no matter if this book is successful or not, I was walking in your shoes before I wrote it.

This brings me to my promise. At the beginning of this book, I promised you that I would tell you a secret. And if you decide today to make a change, my secret will be your boost and will give you more confidence that you can change, that you can start over, that you have a chance even if you can't yet see the light at the end of the tunnel.

When I had the idea for this book, I was dealing with some difficulties in my life. I'd suffered one too many knockouts at that point. But the most recent truly left me feeling alone and stuck. I'd lost my company, I'd lost my girl, and worst and most seriously of all, I'd lost myself. I felt like I was three hundred pounds overweight and stuck.

Despite all this, I was offered a great opportunity I had wanted for a long time. So, despite all this weight on me, I grabbed it with both hands. Things didn't go as smoothly in the beginning as I'd expected, but my ability to adapt quickly had people pretty surprised, including myself.

But that's not what made me understand my true potential. That change came on the day I came to work after a "snow night" with no sleep and a hangover.

I felt like a loser and wanted to give up, despite the fact that I'd just overseen a big change at work. I'd made the place come alive. With the help of the chef, I'd added new dishes to the menu. I trusted myself, and things were looking good. In less than three weeks of me taking over with a new menu, we started to match weekend numbers on weekdays and managed a big jump on weekends.

However, I felt up and down about everything. Mostly down if I'm honest, as I still felt bad about losing everything that I had the year before. I'd had a big opportunity to go my own way, leaving my partners. They were shocked, but I felt it was time for me to move on. They managed to persuade me to stay. Even though my head knew that leaving was the right thing, my heart wouldn't let me go because I didn't want to let them down. Here is a tip for life from what I've learned: *when you need to make any decisions in your life, when one side of you doesn't agree, try not to make sudden changes or decisions.*

When you make a decision that either your heart or mind doesn't agree with, you will fail. In the end, I lost my company, I lost my clients when my partner took all of them, and on top of it all, I lost the girl who I thought was the one!

Back to that night that changed everything. As I mentioned, my feelings about the past, combined with a long night, meant I was very moody at work. One of my employees came to me and said something that changed my life. Isn't it amazing how sometimes things just click because of something someone says, or something you read just resonates ...?

Her name was Vicky. She said, "Z, don't you see how much power you have here on us? How you feel affects everyone."

Then it hit me! My *whole life* hit me! And things started to make sense. All my life, I couldn't understand what I was doing wrong. Why were people so afraid of me? Especially those who had more than me? More money, more girls, better families, and more support. How could it be that all of those so-called friends were so afraid of some guy who thought he had nothing?

Well, the thing is I had it all. I just didn't believe it. So, when a girl or guy or family would tell me how good-looking I was, I always thought they were my friends, so they had to say that. There was something magical about Vicky's words that made all those feelings of self-doubt suddenly disappear. The next day, I woke up, washed my face, and was ready to go, ready to learn about myself.

Things didn't work out with that new opportunity, but this time I didn't mind, because by then I had my own company and a business idea that I knew would be golden once I found the right investor.

And then, COVID-19 struck, and everything stopped! Clients stopped paying me, the city was in lockdown, and I needed to move from my apartment in Soho. But, like so many of us, I saw it as an opportunity. I knew all the developers were going to be home on their computers, so I thought, *OK, I will email all of them daily until someone gives me a chance.*

I started to look for ways to shift my thoughts, forgive my past, and forgive myself for my mistakes. It wasn't easy. It hurt like laser treatment! It took me a few months, but with meditation and books to guide and inspire me to want to know more, I was able to overcome it.

Out of the blue, things got better. My ex-girlfriend called me on Facetime and apologized for what had happened, which

I never could have imagined after how we'd ended things.

I still get negative thoughts, but that's totally normal and part of the human experience. The difference for me now is that I can more easily let them go by doing the following:

- Thanking that thought for trying to help me.
- Then asking for it to *let go* because I am in control now. As strange as it may sound, it works for me.
- I say, "Thank you for this thought. I choose to love this thought, so let go of me."

As I near the end of writing this book, my life is continuing to improve. Business is improving, there is a vaccine for COVID-19, and my industry is back on the rise. Your life can improve too. All you need to do is this:

- Want to be free from your fears.
- Start to believe in yourself.
- Stop seeking approval from others.
- Be the boss of your own life.
- Do good to others and share your success, any way you feel like it.

That wake-up call I had from Vicky enabled me to take the loneliness and anger wrapped up in my broken heart and shift it into the following:

- forgiveness
- self-forgiveness
- self-love
- growth
- manifesting
- workout

- meditation
- open mind
- books
- belief/self-belief
- happiness
- letting go

Remember the Universe gives to those who give to themselves, which means you must focus on you and your gifts to be able to receive from the Universe. Only action can overcome fear and limitations. Don't get pushed around by the fear in your mind. Put fear in its place and be led by the dreams in your heart. Yesterday is the past, today is the present, and tomorrow, who knows if we will wake up? So, start enjoying life and appreciate what you have. Appreciate it as soon as you wake up. Appreciate that morning sun, and appreciate every second you have, because one thing is for sure: it's all going to end someday.

I'm going to repeat myself a little here so I can really drum it into your mind!

Here are the questions:

- Do you want it?
- Do you want to change?
- Do you want to be happy?
- Do you want to feel fulfilled?
- Do you want to see the opportunities in front of you?
- Are you able to take responsibility for your life?
- Are you ready to take responsibility for your actions?
- Are you ready to start loving yourself and believing in you?
- Are you ready to face your fears?
- Are you ready to face yourself?

If your answers are yes, then next I ask, "How *badly* do you want it?" Because if you want it badly enough, you can make huge changes, just like me.

And when you do, you can write to me (please do!) and say, "Yes, I was there. I've done that, and look at me now! Just look. At. Me."

Now it's only fair to warn you that just because you have shifted toward a happier mindset doesn't mean that nothing bad will ever happen or unexpected issues won't rise again. They will. That's just how life goes! But now you know we were made to make mistakes so we can learn and grow and shape ourselves according to those mistakes. Life isn't just happy moments, but a positive mindset and understanding that these challenges allow us to grow sure help us to get over those challenges faster. So, remember to be humble and grateful, and thank the Universe for the life challenges it puts in front of us. Those challenges will make you a stronger, better person.

So, here it is. The secret I promised to tell you, the secret that makes up the law of attraction.

The law of attraction is

- happy thoughts, gratitude, forgiveness, and letting go of the past
- forgiving yourself for your mistakes, doing good, saying thank you for money coming in and money going out
- manifesting what you want, meditating, shifting thoughts from how a bad a situation is to how you can make it into a good one
- seeing the positive in every give and take

- believing in yourself and minding your own business, cutting people off who are toxic, and helping yourself so you can help others

What will happen if you complete all of those steps?

I can tell you that after eight months of working on myself, this whole law of attraction of manifesting energy works! I am proof of that. This book is proof of that. The fact you are reading this means you are helping manifest my dream to help others who need food, education, or books for school. This book's profit in the end will help raise money for children or homeless people. So even if you don't personally find my book of value, you can still be happy with your purchase, because you've donated to a good cause.

Now go and get your nose out of this book and start putting what you've learned into practice. Pass it on to someone who needs it and move forward to a new you, a new day, and a new beginning.

And fuck your past!

Peace and love to you.

Suggested Reading

The Universe Has Your Back by Gabby Bernstein

Spiritual Attraction by Gabby Bernstein

Teach Yourself to Meditate by Eric Harrison

Real Happiness by Sharon Salzberg

Peace from Within by Thea Faye

One Small Step Can Change Your Life by Robert Maurer

Happy Money by Ken Honda

I am deeply grateful to
Alethea Lawton and Michelle Wanasundera
for their immeasurable help.
Without their support, this book
would not have been complete.